THE
FUTURE
OF THE
OFFICE

PETER CAPPELLI

THE
FUTURE
OF THE
OFFICE

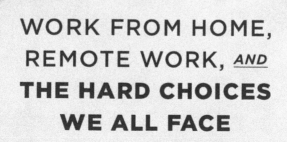

WORK FROM HOME,
REMOTE WORK, *AND*
THE HARD CHOICES
WE ALL FACE

WHARTON
SCHOOL
PRESS

Published by Wharton School Press
The Wharton School
University of Pennsylvania
3620 Locust Walk
300 Steinberg Hall-Dietrich Hall
Philadelphia, PA 19104
Email: whartonschoolpress@wharton.upenn.edu
Website: wsp.wharton.upenn.edu

Ebook ISBN: 978-1-61363-136-2
Paperback ISBN: 978-1-61363-153-9
Hardcover ISBN: 978-1-61363-154-6

Contents

Introduction

By 2005, Google had become the top choice of college graduates as the place to work. Its new office buildings were renowned for the employee perks: gourmet food for breakfast, lunch, and dinner; concierge service; bring your dog to work; spaces for napping—you name it.

The fact that it had such terrific benefits had a purpose—to keep employees at the office. This was not only because they would be working more, but also because their interactions with each other sparked new ideas and innovations that were incredibly valuable to the company.[1] Tech companies and a great many organizations saw this approach of getting people into the office and keeping them there as a best practice.

Yet in May 2021, Google announced a sharp shift in the other direction. Twenty percent of employees could work from home permanently, and another 20% could work remotely, tied to a series of Google locations elsewhere. The remaining 60% could work someplace other than their office two days a week; and for four weeks out of the year, they could work anywhere in the world.[2]

The takeaway: Get the workforce out of the office.

After a year and a half of offices being shut down and employees working from home because of the COVID-19 pandemic, white-collar work all over the world is facing a fundamental inflection point for its future. Evidence and anecdotes say that many of those employees like working remotely and that businesses survived, and in some cases thrived. Unlike Google, many employers largely want to return to how things were before the pandemic, while most employees want to maintain the flexibility they have grown to value.

We now face a big question: What is the future of the office? Should we all go back to the physical space and the way things were, should we continue to stay home, or should we do something different?

Forget the fascination with other topics that dominate when we talk about the "future of work," such as what artificial intelligence might ultimately do to work, our obsession with trivial differences in the attitudes of generations, and other imagined issues. Working from home could change more about office work than anything in a century, it is upon us right now, and we have to choose fast.

It sounds very sensible to go back to the office and pick up where we left off. We've been doing office work for hundreds of years, and we've figured out ways to manage problems and get things done there. We had a temporary break in the action that was a little longer than we predicted, but that will soon be over. Let's get back to work.

On the other hand, it sounds equally sensible not to go back. Office employees generally liked working from home. Employers, remarkably, report that on balance things worked no worse and maybe even better with remote work. We've been at this for a year and a half. Why go back?

Then there's the third option: something that incorporates office work and remote work and tries to make everyone happy. The wide variety of options here is what is known as a hybrid approach, but exactly what that means can vary dramatically from one organization to another.

There was no choice during the COVID-19 pandemic. It forced a giant (and unwanted) experiment of having to work from home. It began as a speed bump, akin to a series of snow days for schoolchildren, then quickly turned into a longer-term event, as we might expect in recoveries from natural disasters. It then became a kind of new normal. In most cases, white-collar workers ended up working from home for well over a year with no time to plan for how to do so.

Now, there is time to think through what to do. Keeping things as they are means working from home almost entirely. As of the summer of 2021, most of the US restrictions on staying home have been lifted. We can think more carefully about the path to take, employer by employer. But we have to choose.

This decision has huge implications for individuals, for employers, and for society. There are advocates on all sides. Depending on whom you ask, it is a means of liberating people from office life, of reducing car commuting and pollution, or of destroying the commercial real-estate market and center cities and making it impossible to get away from work.

This could be the moment to redefine what work means for employees and how it fits into society. It could also be an opportunity to make a big and costly mistake. It could be that the work-from-home experience during the pandemic was unique and will not translate to a more "normal" period.

The problem is that it is not at all clear what we should do. Not everyone liked working from home, and there were a lot of other things going on besides working remotely that might not be replicated going forward. The experience where everyone had to be home is quite unlike the hybrid approaches most employers refer to now. There are potential arrangements where some people are in the office and others are not, where some people get to choose whether to be in the office or at home, and where some people are remote permanently. All have different and important implications.

A Cultural Touchpoint at Stake

"The office" has been a permanent fixture in white-collar work for centuries. It is not just the place where work gets done but also the center of work-related intrigue, office politics, and public failures and successes. It is a source for literature, movies, and eponymous

TV shows. Among other things, a remarkable 22% of all married couples have reported in recent years that they met and started dating at their offices.[3] *New York* magazine's May 2021 issue is an elegy to the office, documenting with personal anecdotes how intertwined its changes have been with our social lives and the experience of that city over the past 100 years. Given how much time we spend at work, getting rid of offices raises profound questions about social isolation if we retreat to our homes for work and for everything else.

Then there is the economic impact. Employers spend huge amounts of money on offices, in part showing off with corporate campuses, towering buildings, and individual offices designed to reflect and convey prestige on employees. The practice of counting ceiling tiles to see whose office was bigger has been a standard part of judging status. A lot of money went to basic amenities like bathrooms and ventilation systems but also to designs that were supposed to stimulate performance: breakout rooms to encourage informal meetings, interior designs to facilitate collaboration, and quiet rooms for individual tasks. A move away from offices would be a crisis for the $1.7 trillion office real-estate industry, the $600 billion construction industry, and all the businesses and employees that serve office jobs.

But office work also creates commuting, which has much less of a case for redeeming value as it costs time and money and pollutes. Two-career couples and the demands of raising children create enormous tensions by keeping parents in the office longer and away from their children and their needs. Working from home has the possibility to end the former and solve the latter.

We have very little time to think through these issues, but we must do so quickly.

It is easy to forget, and many commentators have, that remote work in the form of telecommuting (as it was known then) was the hot topic throughout the 1990s. We have quite an extensive body of research evidence as to how things went, especially for employees. What is important about that context is that it is very much like the hybrid models we are considering again, and less like the "all-in, everyone is home" experience we will likely leave behind after the pandemic. That research (which I'll outline in chapter 2) shows possible benefits for employers but a worse picture for remote employees than we are imagining for the future.

It is worth considering carefully why the interest in telecommuting faded so quickly, from being a dominant topic in the business press in 2000 to virtually disappearing by 2007. Silicon Valley companies such as Google created the new norm that extended the dominance of the office with new and huge investments in office space and related support systems designed not only to help performance but to keep employees in the office. Office footprints and the investments in them got bigger and more entrenched.

Now it could be gone, just like that.

What's the Reason for the Shift?

What do we make of the switcheroo by companies like Google, which, like other companies I'll talk about, is pushing employees out yet also still planning to spend billions on a new campus in San Jose, California?

Was "the Office" a Mistake All Along?

One interpretation is that the previous way of doing things was simply wrong. Not only was trying to keep everyone in the office longer a bad idea, but the whole idea of being in an office may have been a mistake. If it is true that not only are people happier but offices are more effective if no one is in them, then that is a profound revocation of centuries of practice. All the effort in the past hundred years to design offices, to provide amenities to support employees, as well as all the research and practice about the importance of face-to-face interactions and communication—all of that is bested just by leaving people alone. That would be a remarkable conclusion.

Maybe the Pandemic Was a Unique Situation for Work Too

Another interpretation is that a lot of other things were going on during the pandemic that made it unique. Business results were far better than expected, in large part because of the unprecedented amount of federal money and support for businesses flowing through the economy. Many companies reported that the nature of the work they did during the pandemic was more "nuts and bolts" and less innovative than in normal times, when having everyone away from the office would have been a much bigger liability. The fact that employees were staring down a terrible situation—possibly being sick themselves, stuck at home taking care of kids and family *and* without a job or income—made the ability to work from home a blessing that demanded extra efforts to keep their organizations and jobs going.

The most important "other" factor, which gets very little attention, is that almost all companies trusted their employees—perhaps because they had no choice—and could let up on the "face time" model and micromanagement, focusing more on what employees were actually accomplishing. Smart employers asked their employees for help, and the ones that had been good to their employees got it. Can that be replicated going forward?

Or Do Employees Have Options, and Employers Know It?

Finally, a third interpretation of the move away from the office that companies like Google have made might be that having had a taste of not being in the office all the time, employees have decided that they want to keep working from home. If Google wouldn't give it to them, someone else would.

The genie is out of the bottle, at least for employees with opportunities. Those employees may end up paying a price for staying out of the office, but it will be hard to get them back to the office full-time, at least for a while. It may be better for employers to move to some remote-work options before other employers offer them the alternative of staying home.

Why I Wrote This Book

I have been studying the workplace for more than a generation, especially the practices employers use to manage employees. In the process, I have been documenting changes in those practices: how we hire, how we manage performance, and more.

Every year over the past decade or so, there have been claims that some reasonably modest change will soon constitute "the new normal." I have spent some time knocking those claims down. There is no doubt, though, that the shutdown of office work for a year and a half is a profound change, the likes of which the workplace has never seen. If someone had told us in March 2020 that we would be staying home and wouldn't return to the office for more than a year, it would have sounded impossible. How would the economy and society survive?

It will take a long time before we truly understand how we adjusted and got work done. In the meantime, we have to decide what to do. What we have so far is not only conflicting advice but conflicting evidence. We need a sober account of how things actually went during the pandemic, as good as we can get now, and we need to consider the reasonably extensive evidence we already had about remote working. That is what I try to do in this book. There are many options between all remote work and all on-site work. The choices this time really could constitute a new normal. Knowing how to choose is a pressing topic.

In chapter 1, I review what the experience of the pandemic has been. There are many caveats, the most important being that the information we have is still based mostly on opinion and extrapolation. But it is hard not to see the evidence we have as stunningly supportive of working from home, especially for employees but even for employers. The most pressing question is how well the unique, nationwide, and company-wide experience of the pandemic would translate to the hybrid models under consideration where offices remain open and employees can choose where to work.

At a minimum, many observers see the push to working at home as a kind of liberation for employees, being free from the restrictions and pressures of the office and a better way to balance work and life conflicts. It also opens up the possibility to live wherever you want, even if your employer is not based there. More skeptical observers, which include me, see that the push to get rid of the office could slide toward even more arm's-length arrangements: People can work when they want, where they want, but as independent contractors—not employees.

The fact that employees want something like the ability to work from home is not new, and simply wanting something does not mean it will happen. Employers hold virtually all the cards in the United States. Whether things change depends on their interests. That is why much of the focus of this book is on their decisions.

In chapter 1, I examine what we can take away and what we cannot from the recent evidence about operating during the pandemic. That's followed by the more serious evidence in chapter 2 from research on the surprisingly common remote work arrangements before the pandemic and its effects, which have not been so positive for remote workers. Chapter 3 describes what employers get out of remote work, a conclusion dominated by real-estate savings but also by the possibility that mobile employees with options will change the labor market and force employers to respond to hybrid models that are more sensitive to employee interests.

We are at one of those important inflection points that have often followed pandemics. The office is ground zero for it. Right now, companies are all over the place: Facebook, Twitter, and other tech companies have said many employees will work remotely on a permanent basis. Goldman Sachs, JP Morgan, and others have said it is important for everyone to come back to the office. Ford has redone its office space so that most employees can work from home at least part of the time. And GM has planned to let local managers work out arrangements on an ad hoc basis.

There is no consensus. The story is clearly fluid, which means we are still deciding.

As we will see, some of those positions have already gone by the wayside. Most are waiting to see what everyone else is going to do—a sensible strategy, except everyone cannot do that, and in this case, waiting and continuing on is choosing.

It is possible that we may have more time than we think to decide what to do about work-from-home options, unfortunately, because the pandemic may not end with a bang. Resistance to vaccination will result in individuals continuing to contract the virus. New strains of the virus may get around the current vaccines, or the protection provided by those vaccines may be short-lived, among other potential unforeseen issues, in which case important aspects of pandemic quarantining and working from home may continue. The odds of this may be lower than they once seemed, but it is a scenario worth considering.

Epidemiologists warn that it is possible that a new pathogen could result in another shutdown. Given that this is not a new concern, it is worth asking why virtually no employers in the United States had any kind of plan as to what to do in the event of a pandemic. That might not sound surprising—who could have known? But a decade earlier, a great many employers, including my own, did have contingency plans for handling a pandemic, sparked by the possibility that the 2009 swine flu might surge into something truly threatening to society. We had protocols for working remotely just in case. Why that didn't happen this time is worth considering, as are the lessons we should learn going forward.

The final concern, which is shorter term, is that government regulations in many locations still limit employers' ability to bring back employees and, if they do bring them back, how they can do it. Employers that are permitted to have employees on-site have to retrofit their offices to conform to safety protocols including spacing (fewer desks and more space between them), higher-volume HVAC systems, shields between employees who are closer together, and restrictions on elevator capacity. Is the cost of retrofitting offices for what might well prove to be a temporary period worth it? My sense is that most employers believe it is not and are putting off bringing employees back until all those restrictions are lifted. As soon as restrictions lift, though, employers will face the same choices.

In chapter 4, I consider how to bring employees back to the office, assuming that happens. Having been away for a year and a half, in some cases longer, returning may be a more novel experience than we expect. It is also an opportunity to change the way we work, which I cover in chapter 5. If we do not seize this opportunity immediately, the moment will pass.

What I try to do in this volume is lay out the facts and arguments about the policies and practices associated with remote work. I do not provide an exhaustive list of the issues. There is, for example, a wide body of knowledge about how individual leaders and managers should handle the interpersonal issues with remote work, and many of the psychological challenges that remote workers have are addressed elsewhere.[4]

But the place to start is whether and how to organize remote work. What problem do we want it to solve, and what do we know about how it works?

Chapter 1

The COVID-19 Experience
What We Can (and Can't) Learn from It

In April 2020, an ABC News correspondent committed what under normal circumstances would be a career-ending move. Like many TV reporters during the pandemic, he was doing a segment from his home. When the camera pulled back from a close-up, however, it revealed that he was not wearing pants. A few people noticed, they tweeted about it, the segment went viral, and then everyone knew.

He responded by saying that he was actually just multitasking and already had his gym shorts on, which is where he was going right after that segment. He treated it as a joke, making fun of himself. Fortunately for him, most Americans thought it *was* funny, perhaps because they, too, did not bother wearing pants in the many Zoom meetings in which they suddenly found themselves, and his star rose.[5] It was a signal that the norms about working from home had changed.

The circumstances of working from home during the pandemic were certainly unusual. It is crucial to learn what we can about how things worked, though, because that experience is what is driving the interest in keeping it going. The reports from the trenches indicate that it went surprisingly well, arguably remarkably well, as described in this chapter. The work-from-home experience during the pandemic could well be better than what studies found in earlier periods, in part because we have much better video communication.

In the United States, the most important pandemic before COVID-19 was the so-called Spanish Flu of 1918, which killed

50 million worldwide (compared with 17 million from World War I). One-quarter of the US population got the flu, and roughly 675,000 died from it—six-tenths of 1% of the population, including my grandmother. As of June 2021, this percentage is roughly four times more than the US population that has died from complications of COVID-19.

What changed as a result of that pandemic that might give us some clues as to what might persist after the COVID-19 experience? It saw many of the same decentralized responses and local battles between the public health concern of shutting down with quarantines and business concerns with keeping things open. Many cities imposed ordinances requiring that masks be worn in public: San Francisco fined first-time offenders $5, and subsequent offenders a substantial amount. New York City enlisted Boy Scouts to hand out warning cards to people they saw spitting.[6] There were also protests against these regulations. Extensive efforts during the pandemic to discourage people from kissing and shaking hands had some effect, but it did not last long. Neither did the fear of urban areas where infection risks were greater. Cities boomed when it ended. The Roaring Twenties followed.

The most important long-term effect of the Spanish Flu happened in the labor market. The infection disproportionately affected men, killing far more men than women and leaving others with lingering disabilities. This outcome created opportunities for women, especially jobs in factories that had been the preserve of men.[7] As with the COVID-19 pandemic, businesses that relied on face-to-face interactions, like restaurants and hotels, were hit especially hard. But they came back. What we did not see then were offices operating remotely.

How Expectations Changed during COVID-19

The ramp-up period from taking COVID-19 seriously in the United States, roughly early March 2020, to the shutdown orders later that month was quite short. Before the shutdown orders were issued, the public discussion suggested that it might take 14 days to "stop the spread." Employers had very little time to plan, but it also did not seem all that important because it was not supposed to last long. In many places, the beginning of the pandemic was viewed as something that would be over soon, like an extended snowstorm.

When those state and municipal shutdown orders first came, though, they were for much longer than anticipated—not weeks but months. Still, we generally thought that we would be more or less back to normal by Memorial Day.

The initial responses from employers focused on the finances of a temporary stoppage and not on how to keep working. Marriott International, part of the hard-hit hotel industry, announced that two-thirds of its corporate staff would be furloughed—a layoff with the expectation of recall—for two months, still receiving 20% of their pay. Remaining employees took a 20% pay cut. Other corporate employees took temporary leave.[8]

Companies like Amazon and Walmart that continued to operate, and where almost all employees were on-site, were initially quite generous to employees. They offered employees bonuses and the option to stay home (albeit without pay) if they were afraid of contracting the virus at work. Around June, though, most of that generosity stopped. Whether it was because the employers could see that continuing this indefinitely was going to be expensive or because of some other reason is not clear.[9]

By the end of May, it was clear that the pandemic was not in retreat, but there was some expectation that it might lift in the summer of 2020. Some employers targeted Labor Day for "reopening." But Microsoft shocked the business community by announcing that it would not reopen its offices until the summer of 2021, almost a year later. One of the wake-up calls from Microsoft's experience was how school closings made it impossible for many working parents to get child care and return to the office, even if it was safe for them to do so. The spillover effects with family issues had never been so clear.

Because we had no idea of the length of the pandemic and associated shutdowns, few organizations thought about it as a learning exercise. As a result, they were not keeping track of how things were going, in part because everything was done so quickly and often on the fly.

It's also true, unfortunately, that only a few organizations had a good idea about employee job performance before the pandemic. Organizations do track financial performance and overall business outcomes, both of which were often good in the pandemic. But as to what is happening at the level of the individual employee, we probably know less about that now than we did a generation ago. As a quirky example, some surveys find employees reporting that relationships with their supervisors actually improved during the pandemic. Was that simply because they saw them less? A more positive explanation is that some companies mandated that their supervisors check in with all their remote subordinates, which would appear to be more actual contact than they had in the office.

The pandemic and associated shutdown was bad news for almost all employees. One estimate indicates that 20 million people in the United States lost their jobs just in the first month of the pandemic.[10] By May 2020, a staggering 50 million people—almost one-third of the labor force—reported that they had been unable to work during the previous month because of the pandemic,[11] although many of those remained "employed." Gross domestic product fell by 3.5%; however, some estimates suggest that the loss compared with where the economy would have been without the pandemic was more than double that amount.[12] Keeping their jobs, and their organizations afloat, provided a lot of motivation for employees to work hard.

A Gigantic Shift

Government statistics report that at the peak of the pandemic, 35% of employees worked completely from home.[13] If we ask what proportion of employees whose jobs could have been done remotely ended up working from home, the figure is over 70%. This was not what we are now calling a hybrid model. Employees were not choosing whether to work from home. Most everyone whose job allowed remote work and was not "essential" was at home. Unlike in the Great Recession, women were hit harder this time, owing to demands from child care, the need to educate children at home, and more. Overall, 2.4 million women, versus 1.8 million men, dropped out of the labor force between February 2020 and February 2021, which means they were without a job and not looking for a new one.[14] This is a reminder that remote work does not solve all work-life issues.

I was part of the shift to remote work. I went to my office exactly once during the pandemic, and then only to pick up mail.

Not surprisingly, the amount of remote work that happened across industries was driven by how many white-collar jobs they have. Survey results from a February 2021 Harris poll show that the experience of employees varied quite a bit. Twenty-three percent reported that their hours were cut, for example, but 15% said that their hours increased during the pandemic.[15]

A novel entry in this survey is "furloughed," which is something short of a layoff. Eight percent of employees were furloughed as opposed to 11% who were laid off. Furloughed employees have not been separated from the company, and there is an expectation of return. A few companies paid furloughed employees something while they were waiting to be recalled, and the US government allowed those employees to collect unemployment insurance during the pandemic. All told, about 20% of employees were out of work.

There are a great many surveys of employees and their experiences during the pandemic, but one of the most detailed was conducted by Adecco. It surveyed 8,000 full-time office workers early in the pandemic who report that their jobs were altered in important ways, typically by working remotely, across countries. These workers tell a very positive story, with most reporting improved quality of work and of life and well-being. One of the few attributes that got worse was relationships with colleagues.[16]

One of the complications in generalizing from reports that work-from-home had a positive performance is that on-site employees and essential service workers also appeared to perform well during the pandemic, which would seem to suggest that maybe it was rallying around the employer in the crisis that was driving positive outcomes.

The results might also be different depending on when the performance was measured. Did performance drop once the novelty wore off? We know that US companies backed off from some of the support they provided early in the pandemic once it became clear that the shutdown could go on for a very long time. Having said that, many surveys report similar results, suggesting that performance was no worse and on average was arguably better during 2020.

When asked the more basic question as to whether they thought the whole work-from-home exercise had been a success, employers in a PwC survey were more likely to say so than employees, 83% versus 71%.[17] An assessment like this may well depend on expectations, and employers may have anticipated it would be worse for business than the employees thought it would be for them personally. It is difficult to have imagined in March 2020 that we would have a stock market boom during a pandemic year.

A further complication in interpreting the positive results from employers and employees is that another factor that affects job performance was going on along with working from home. In addition to giving employees more control over their work, working from home also created a sense of obligation among employees. Employees understood that while working from home was necessary for the employer, it was also a considerable accommodation for the employees who would otherwise be out of work, as 20 million Americans were. Employers also invested a great deal of trust in the work-from-home relationship, giving employees control and trusting that they would get the work done.

Researchers have long known the power of the norm of reciprocity in the workplace. Behavioral science refers to this as social exchange: Employers take care of employees, and the employees feel an obligation to respond by taking care of the employer's interests.

Not all employer surveys suggested that things went well, however. A study conducted in the United Kingdom (UK), Europe, and Asia found that about two-thirds of companies said that staff morale had suffered during the pandemic.[18] Nor is it clear what is being measured when we ask for opinions as to how working from home went. "Better" and "worse" are shaped by previous circumstances.

When we turn to more objective measures, one of the arguments for remote work by employers is that the savings from not having to commute to work will allow employees to work longer. There is some evidence of this from a study of a call center in China, which I discuss in chapter 2, and from a study by the company Prodoscore, whose business is measuring and monitoring employee productivity in IT jobs. The studies found some evidence that performance was up during the pandemic—but so were hours, about one additional hour per day in January 2021 data than before the pandemic.[19] But not all studies find that. A recent and careful study of higher-skilled employees in IT services during the pandemic found that while performance held steady during the work-from-home period, hours of work rose by about 30%. In other words, productivity fell. Data from workforce analytics software found that employees spent more time in meetings than before the shutdown and that those with children worked longer hours than childless employees.[20]

Figure 1.1 details how the time saved from not commuting was split between work and nonwork activities.

A "New Normal" or an "Aberration"?

After initial indications from companies about permanent moves toward working from home, we saw some walking back of that enthusiasm. While Facebook has been one of the leaders in advocating permanent remote work for at least some employees, CEO Mark Zuckerberg has been more circumspect recently on longer-term performance issues. For example, he estimated that half of his employees "really just wanted to get back to the office as soon as possible," and he pointed out the loss of working without in-person connections. "It's unclear at this point whether we're just all drafting off of existing bonds that have developed before it started," he said.[21]

Figure 1.1. How Remote Workers Allocated Additional Time

Where additional time was allocated when working from home, August 2020 (%)

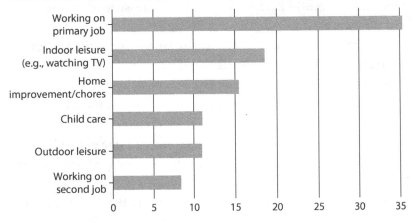

Source: *Becker Friedman Institute*, Wall Street Journal.

Goldman Sachs CEO David Solomon articulated that same sense: "For a business like ours, which is an innovative, collaborative apprenticeship culture, this is not ideal for us. And it's not a new normal. It's an aberration that we're going to correct as soon as possible."[22]

One of the very few companies reporting on a systematic effort to learn how work had changed with the new work-from-home approach was Microsoft, albeit in one small part of the organization.[23] The team found that the number of meetings (on Zoom) increased, but that they were shorter compared with office meetings, with an evolving norm of 30 minutes. They also found a surge of work roughly after the dinner hour, perhaps driven by families whose children settled down with after-dinner activities. Work blurred into weekends more so than before the pandemic. They also found some groups taking active measures to protect individual time, such as having no meetings on Fridays. One of the surprising conclusions, given the apparent benefits of working from home to family life, seems to be the extent to which remote work appeared to intrude into what had been clearer work-life boundaries before the pandemic.

Stanford professor Robert Sutton reported how remote work is evolving, using the example of new Zoom etiquette that was developed to make remote work more civil. Specifically, he observed sidebar conversations in the chat function, some of which are interesting (especially when people forget to mark their message as private), most of which are distracting. He pointed out that smarter groups reach agreement up front to avoid those private chats going forward.[24]

Aside from hours worked, is it actually easier to work from home, as opposed to just being more convenient and avoiding commuting time? It is true that we can sleep in until just before our meetings, and we only have to look presentable from the waist up, but there are other, unique problems with working from home, as figure 1.2 indicates.

Advocates for the "new normal" view of remote work rightly note that video conferencing is far better than what we had in the period before COVID-19, but it remains the case that we are nevertheless dependent on technology across many more people. When

Figure 1.2. What About Remote Work Went Poorly?

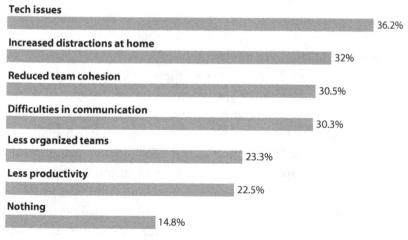

Tech issues — 36.2%
Increased distractions at home — 32%
Reduced team cohesion — 30.5%
Difficulties in communication — 30.3%
Less organized teams — 23.3%
Less productivity — 22.5%
Nothing — 14.8%

Source: Wall Street Journal, survey from Upwork of 1,500 hiring managers, April 2020.

an entire team is working remotely, meetings are dependent on everyone's internet service, everyone's home computer, and everyone's ability to keep their software updated and understand how to use it. Tech issues, the number one problem in the survey in figure 1.2, are not eliminated by better software. The issue of tech security when we distribute all aspects of work remotely has remained largely out of public discussion, but it gives security experts fits.

A further complication in knowing the true effects of remote work during the pandemic is that we did not have a great sense of how well things worked previously. Suppose, for example, we see results saying that employees thought that Zoom meetings worked just as well as in-person meetings. But we also know that, before the pandemic, most employees thought most meetings were a waste of time because they were poorly run, unnecessary, or both.[25] The appropriate conclusion is not that there is nothing to be gained from in-person meetings; it is that we run our meetings so poorly that it does not matter whether they are on Zoom or in person.

What's in It for the Employer? They're Taking Back Your Office

The headline announced the future: "The Office Citadel Crumbles." The accompanying story described how companies were using new technology to get people out of the office, reduce the corporate real-estate footprint, and save money in the process, in 1995.[26]

The work-from-home push was the result of an effort to cut office real estate. How employees might manage the switch to working from home came later. It began with a cost-cutting wave starting in the 1980s and the pressure to improve shareholder value. Real estate became a hot-button issue in that effort once companies realized how much capital they had tied up in unproductive offices, warehouses, and other locations.[27]

Office space began to shrink. The size of a typical office fell by about one-third from the 1970s through the early 2010s, and cubicles shrank in size by 25%–50% over the 1980s.[28] Companies also redesigned their office spaces to make them more standardized and modular so that they could downsize quickly and cheaply.[29] But empty offices were another matter altogether. An empty office—even a small one—gave the appearance that the company was wasting money on office space.

This insight was not lost on employees who operated in the field. The first and simplest response was to get rid of those offices altogether. IBM claimed to have cut real estate costs by 75% in one division by having the consulting employees telecommute. (This was the beginning of the joke that "IBM" no longer stood for "I've been moved." It now meant "I'm by myself," as corporate relocations gave way to telecommuting.) By 2009, IBM claimed to have 40% of its employees working remotely and said it was saving $100 million in real-estate costs as a result.[30]

AT&T moved 10,000 account executives to virtual status, taking back their offices; Dun & Bradstreet cut its Dallas office space by half with technology that allowed its sales force to work remotely. Ernst & Young cut its New York office by 40% by pushing its consultants out into the field and taking away their permanent offices.[31] Looking at the inefficiency of empty offices, one set of observers concluded that by 2000, most employees would not have offices at all.[32]

Not all offices can be eliminated for employees who are not in that space every day. Even consultants and sales reps need to be back in the office for meetings and to see clients. This is one contemporary definition of a "hybrid" model, where employees work remotely some days but are in the office other days. The problem from the employer's side is that an empty office costs about as much as an occupied one.

The way around this was the novel idea that you could have an office when you wanted to come in, but it wouldn't be your own office. This is known as "hoteling": an employee who came into the office would have a temporary space, similar to guests at a hotel. The idea is as simple as asking five employees who are out of the office most of the time to share an office, cutting space down from five offices to one. The idea of "sharing" an office seems very unprofessional, though—five little desks jammed into the same office like graduate students? Instead, employers keep one generic office with one desk. Employees can "reserve" it when they will be in town, like a hotel. If we get fancy, or we expect the visiting employees to need to see clients in that shared office, we allow each of the five to personalize it with their own pictures, desk toys, and so on, which we bring out and set up whenever they are coming in.

Many companies tried something like this, but Ernst & Young seems to have pioneered it in 1993 with its consultants in its New York office. The problem with this approach, noted by most observers, is the supply chain challenge: If all the virtual employees show up at the same time, there will not be enough desks for all of them.

The high-water mark, and eventually the low mark as well, for hoteling and remote work in general came at the Chiat advertising agency, a powerhouse in its creativity and business success. Jay Chiat, the head of the agency and the all-powerful boss, had an insight that the physical structure of the office was both unnecessary and stifling of creativity. So, he designed new office space, first in the New York location and then in Los Angeles, with two profound innovations that are quite relevant to this work-from-home moment.

The first was to give all the employees laptops and cell phones and tell them that they could work virtually, wherever and whenever they wanted. The second was to create an extreme version of an open office: no private space, no desks. Employees had lockers where they could store personal things. Instead of desks, there were clusters of couches and tables, a central gathering place, conference rooms, and a bizarre set of Tilt-A-Whirl domed cars taken from old amusement-park rides, where two people could sit down together and brainstorm.

Critics loved the building and the ideas behind it, and it received enormous attention. Employees did not love it. The sense was that people did not get much work done when they were away from the office. The shared space in the office proved to be a source of competition as employees staked out the choice locations. They also hoarded office supplies and equipment rather than returning them when they were finished. Because there was no private space, people in the Los Angeles office used their cars to store files and other materials, running out to the parking lot to get documents and other things when they needed them. In short, the open office appeared to foster competition instead of collaboration.

When the agency was sold, the new owners soon put back offices for the executives, added a desk and landline phone for everyone, and tried to create an environment to get people to stay in the office.[33]

Despite the Chiat office implosion, interest in hoteling and telecommuting did not immediately fade. Fueled by the potential of the internet to make remote work easier, forecasts at the turn of the millennium suggested that a quarter or more of US workers could be telecommuting by 2006.[34]

But neither did it take off as expected. A 2000 *Wall Street Journal* article argued that employers were backing away from it even then. It concluded that the enthusiasm for it was driven in part by the tight labor market—shortage of office space but also candidates wanting to work in the office. As the market started to cool, so did the interest in virtual work.[35] Midway through the first decade of the twenty-first century, *CIO Magazine* reporter Thomas Wailgum suggested that virtual work and hoteling in particular had simply vanished.[36]

Some companies still use at least some form of hoteling. Almost all companies with multiple locations allow managers from other offices to "plug in" when they are traveling or nearby. Consulting companies where employees spend most of their time with clients in different locations use it in part so that the employees can have a base in those locations when they need one. But it appears that the initial interest in hoteling cooled off sharply. There is no definitive reason as to why that happened, but it is fair to say that most employees like having their own office, and senior employees who lost theirs had some ability to make a fuss. If I am coming into the office to see my coworkers, and they are spread all over the building with hoteling, I am unlikely to bump into them. We need to make an appointment to see each other, and the fact that we might all have a temporary space in the same location is no more convenient than meeting at Starbucks.

If you are an employer whose plan for the future relies on hoteling, it is worth thinking about why it faded so quickly. Some companies are ready to try again, or perhaps don't know what happened the first time. HSBC announced in April, for example, that its employees will lose their private offices at its London headquarters in the company's move toward a hoteling model, in which office space will be cut by 40%.[37] Why we should not expect the same result as in the past is not clear.

One reason the interest in hoteling passed might be that many organizations, especially those in tech, moved on to another model that was perhaps even cheaper. In the open office plan, individual offices were done away with in favor of big, open rooms and common tables rather than individual desks.

The justification for such plans was that they increase collaboration, based on research evidence that we tend to interact more with people to whom we are physically close. But the extension of that argument—if we simply squeeze everyone together, we will have more interaction—proves not to be true. Anyone who has worked in an open office plan is familiar with the environment: workers sitting next to each other as in an old library but staring at their own screens and wearing headphones to avoid hearing the conversations around them. We also put up personal barriers through our behavior when there are lots of people in tight quarters, causing such interactions to fall, by a lot.[38] The lack of privacy, of personal space, and of quiet are all reasons employees tend to hate open office plans.

The reason open offices persist is because they are cheaper. They are anathema to pandemic requirements as it is essentially impossible to keep using them and stay compliant with infection restrictions. In fact, a good way to predict which companies will wait until all the restrictions are lifted before bringing back employees is to find out which companies have open offices and still intend to use them.

What to do about office space is an open question. As I'll describe in chapter 2, employees who are out of the office struggle, but it costs almost as much to keep offices open occasionally as it does to keep them open all the time. The cheapest alternative for real estate—permanently remote employees—is also the worst for the employees and their job performance.

Remote Shift: Points to Remember

- Reports on working from home have been remarkably positive, but to paraphrase Samuel Johnson, it isn't so much that we were surprised to see it done well as to see it done at all. It did not seem possible for organizations to even survive with offices shut down for a year and a half.
- Aside from that low bar, it is difficult to make conclusions about how much better individual workers performed, as other factors were motivating performance besides remote work.
- It may be worth the costs for many employees to work from home. Unlike in the pandemic, giving people the choice of where to work creates the problem.
- We should not expect that remote work will solve work-life challenges for employees. The outcome depends on how management executes it.

Chapter 2

Back to the Future
How Remote Work Works

The headline in the *Washington Post* read, "You'll Never Have to Go to Work Again." The article described how innovations in IT make it possible to choose whatever location you want to do your work from. The year was 1969.

The *ability* to work from home is not new. It goes back to pre-industrial England and western Europe in the seventeenth century and the "putting out" system, where workers and their families would take on part of a textile or manufacturing process in their own home, organized by a business merchant. Factories ended this practice with the advantage of centralized capital equipment and the need for workers to be in the factory to use it.

In the United States, remote work for office jobs dates from the Los Angeles smog crisis in the 1970s, when the need to cut air pollution from cars temporarily interrupted commuting to work. Many people had to work from home, which led to the term "telecommuting," since the telephone was the only connection to the office at the time.

With more work being done on computers, which can be taken home, and the fact that the internet and other communications systems do not have to be tied to a particular location, working remotely has become much easier. Instead of "telecommuting," we talk about virtual work or remote work. Estimates suggest that 10% of employees were doing some form of telecommuting in the 1990s. This figure rose to 17% by 2010, and forecasts predicted that a majority of workers would soon be working from home.[39]

Pew Research Center polls indicate that many regular employees were already working from home at some point before the pandemic—as many as 20%, although few of those did so full-time.[40] This figure does not include people who do what is broadly known as "gig" work as independent contractors. This group is not nearly as big a share of the labor force as most observers think, though (only about 6% in US Census data).

Researchers have come at this question from quite different directions. First, during the boom of interest in the 1990s, the big question in the field of management was simply, How does it get done? If you take the person out of the office context, what happens? These studies are a key indicator for the "hybrid" model as we talk about it now, in which some people work remotely but others do not.

The flurry of research about remote work, telecommuting, or virtual offices came right around the turn of the millennium, and it focused on interpersonal issues: What happens to people working remotely and their performance? The conclusion of the vast literature on these employees was, in summary, "not good."[41] They seemed to be worse off in many dimensions associated with their jobs. It was also challenging for supervisors and coworkers to make it succeed.[42]

Perhaps surprisingly, it was not so much working from home that was the issue—it was working from home when everyone else was in the office. This was not the case during the pandemic, when all office workers were home. Thus, paying attention to the research on the telecommunicating period may be more useful than focusing on what people said about their experiences during the pandemic.

The research conclusions apply to people who regularly work remotely, not just those cutting out early on the occasional Friday afternoon. If you are offered the opportunity to continue working from home, should you take it? If you can choose how many hours you want to work from home, what's the right number?

For the Employee: A Few Big Questions

If you have been offered the opportunity to continue working from home, the first and most obvious thing to consider is, if remote work is not being offered to everyone, why are they offering it to me?[43]

We know from people who are away from the office that they lose out on information, especially about opportunities for advancement, because they aren't part of regular, face-to-face conversations at the office. Even if they are getting the same results as their counterparts at the office, those working from home may be less visible to management.

Virtual workers are less likely to feel included in valued activities in the organization and to be part of key strategic decisions than their counterparts who work at the office.[44] If you are not in the office, where the important decisions are made, it is easy to be regarded as someone who is less important, and those labels can become a self-fulfilling prophecy. Given that, if you say yes to remote work, will that be perceived as a signal of weaker commitment to the organization?

We have already heard business leaders make this case, somewhat ungracefully. The CEO of WeWork said that employers will see those who opt to stay home as less committed—the "least engaged" employees—than those who want to come back to the office. (His company provides office space.) The editor of the *Washingtonian*, a monthly magazine, suggested something even tougher: It is easier to lay off people you don't see regularly. She wrote this in a highly visible op-ed while her own staff were working remotely, leading to a one-day strike of those workers.[45]

Who's Going Back?

A related question is, Who will be going back to the office? The more of my peers who will be returning, the worse it will be for me if I stay home. Prior research on remote workers has shown that they are more professionally and socially isolated and, yes, less engaged than those in the office. The more of my peers who go back to the office, the worse my isolation is.[46] Remote workers are likely to miss the face-to-face interaction and informal learning that comes from observing others and networking. Those who telecommute frequently have lower-quality relationships with coworkers, and the more you telecommute, the worse the consequences.[47]

Also, if many of your colleagues are not telecommuting, there is a higher chance you will be perceived as an outlier, as the non-prototypical worker even by your peers. It is easy for team members who are collocated to develop an in-group/out-group mentality, treating those who are physically present better than those who are not present. In fact, some leaders try to create this mentality—the "us against the world" approach—to rally the team around the cause. Professional isolation may detract from worker performance for different reasons, including missing knowledge about appropriate norms or behaviors in the organization as well as contextual knowledge such as how to work with certain clients.

Face time, perhaps unfortunately, matters. Managers tend to attribute more positive personality traits and less negative ones to the employees who spend a lot of time in the office. It is harder for managers to see the hours put in by those working from home, even when they are working longer than their office colleagues. Distance also makes it harder for workers to engage in "impression management," influencing how you are perceived. As the saying goes, those who are out of sight may become out of mind too. A recent study on workers in two large globally distributed product development Fortune 100 companies found that workers who were not located at headquarters had a much harder time signaling their commitment to their manager, and therefore of securing better work opportunities.[48]

To compensate, remote workers find themselves engaging in more impression management to ingratiate themselves, alerting supervisors to their accomplishments and other behavior that looks like self-promotion. These workers find that they need to accept tasks such as projects they don't really want to do as well as meeting at times that are inconvenient for them. In general, they report making more personal sacrifices than their colleagues, volunteering to do extra work or working late hours. The consequence is that remote work ends up taking a toll on employees, particularly in terms of personal sacrifices that often lead to the turnover of these employees or disengagement.

Some developmental experiences and assignments cannot make the transition to virtual work, such as having lunch with an important client. Even though companies may formalize certain trainings that can be easily delivered online, informal development such as mentoring or learning by observing peers is much harder to do outside the office.

As the studies above start to suggest, do I want to be an individual contributor or climb the management ranks? If you want to climb the corporate ladder, the path to the top is still greased by proximity to those in power. A UK government survey before the pandemic found that employees working from home were 40% less likely than their counterparts in the office to be promoted.[49] We see similar negative outcomes in call center studies that I'll outline in a bit. Research has found that you need to be around those in power to get promoted, even if those who work from home perform as well as their counterparts working at the office.[50]

What Kind of Work Am I Doing?

The third question is, What's your role? The easiest tasks to perform remotely are individual contributor roles, because they do not require much interaction with others. Remote workers report greater satisfaction when their work is easily portable across settings, such as when it can be performed independently, without much reliance on other members of the team. The caveat is that jobs like that are also the easiest to turn into contracting positions, and employers have been pushing more jobs in that direction.

If your work involves a project with others, there are many issues to consider. If the rest of the team is on-site, you are more likely to be marginalized. Prior work documented that workers are less likely to respond to team members' messages on time or to provide access to critical data when they are away from the rest of the team.[51] Communication barriers seem to be at the heart of this. Office workers often fail to understand the priorities of their remote peers because it is harder to express those via technology.

One study of distributed teams found that partners working remotely often misinterpreted silence. The study found that silence could mean many different things for different people, ranging from strongly agreeing to strongly disagreeing, or even being ignored.[52] It is hard to know how to interpret it without close-up knowledge. A universal finding in studies on distributed work is that these communication problems end up increasing the time it takes to execute projects. Some information, such as personal issues or problems with coworkers, is just uncomfortable to communicate electronically, as workers may be reluctant to produce a written account of this information. Face-to-face communication is without a doubt the richest communication medium.

It is also easy to face inequities when you are working from home and others are not. One study found that supervisors and coworkers may be more reluctant to call those working from home to solve those last-minute issues because of fear of intruding in their life, turning to those in the office instead.[53] This can create fairness concerns about contributions. Remote teams have more conflicts within the team than do teams in the office because of communication challenges.[54]

Who's My Boss?

The last set of questions is about how I will be managed remotely. Who will be supervising me?

Surprisingly, workers managed by less experienced supervisors may be better off if they are remote, because the biggest drawback of new supervisors is that they tend to micromanage, an aspect that tends to demotivate workers. Micromanaging is much harder to do with remote work. The more complicated the project is, however, the more we need experienced supervisors with the connections to anticipate and solve problems with resources and stakeholders.[55] If you have straightforward tasks, it may be OK to have an inexperienced supervisor. If you are working on something challenging, though, it may well fail without an experienced supervisor. What counts as experience in this case is someone with a lot of connections and information inside the organization so they can find resources and head off problems their remote subordinates can't see.

Finally, how did my employer manage remote work during the pandemic? What direction were they going? It is a bad sign if they spent money on "tattle" software that monitors what employees are doing by watching their computer screens. The main reason people want to work from home is to not be tied to their desks. They can step away and do something important for a few minutes. Software that essentially keeps you from leaving your desk defeats the reason to be home. Prior work has found that the degree of autonomy and of schedule flexibility workers have is an important determinant of the extent to which working from home facilitates work-life balance.[56] If the organization has been monitoring and micromanaging, working from home may not be worth the agita.

It will be much easier to work from home if your employer has gotten clearer and more explicit about performance management—here's what we want you to be doing and how we want to measure it—and if they are requiring supervisors to do more check-ins with remote workers to head off problems.

The Elusive Work-Life Balance

The idea of working from home sounds like a great way to deal with many of the demands of balancing a full-time job and running a household, as so many occasions require that we be in two places at the same time. We can imagine how much easier it would be to manage those conflicts if we could physically be at home and virtually in the office.

There is, of course, another side to having your "office" at home, and that is that your "home" is at the office. We know from prior research that while "home" can provide a respite from the office, it is also the case that we bring our office problems home, and that can disrupt our life there. If we never go home, then there is no getting away from the office. The workday never ends.

Will this happen with remote work? The pre-COVID evidence on this issue is equivocal, and it very much depends on the context, but telecommuting did not appear to make both work and life outside of work better. Trade-offs between the two remain.[57]

Much of the argument for working from home is that cutting commuting will be a real time saver and that the time could be better used elsewhere. No doubt there are people who make constructive use of commuting time, but I suspect most people would prefer to skip it. That says nothing about the cost of commuting as well as the pollution it causes.

There is one caveat to this conclusion, and it reflects the difference between long-run and short-run outcomes. A surprising result from research on transportation shows that every innovation that made it easier to reduce commuting time was met by homeowners deciding to live farther out, seeking commutes that took just as much time but were farther in terms of distance. New highways that made commutes shorter meant that suburbs boomed farther out, keeping commuting time roughly the same.[58] Remote work where employees never come into the office obviously does not have this effect, but the other approaches may. If I have to be in the office only two days a week, I can stand a multihour commute on those two days, something I would have never done five days a week. Employees may well prefer this—otherwise, why did they choose to do so?—but if we think about issues such as pollution and traffic, the benefits would not be quite as sweeping as we imagine.

Other evidence shows that telecommuters take more trips during the day than on-site office workers—they were not simply staying home. They may be driving less in total, depending on the length of their commute, but their time in the car does not drop by as much as the time saved from not having to commute to work.[59]

What happens to the time saved by not commuting? A 2012 study of telecommuting using nationally representative data across decades concluded that it extended working hours for employees, pushed up work demands, and did not lead to any real reduction in work-life conflicts. Seventeen percent of American workers reported that they worked regularly, but not exclusively, at home in 2000, a number that remained roughly unchanged over the next decade, and the average amount of time they worked at home was six hours per week.[60]

To hammer that conclusion, telecommuting was not cutting hours of work, and it was arguably not necessarily cutting hours of work in the office either. This conclusion flags an important definitional problem with telecommuting and the studies of it. The post-pandemic idea of working from home is that being home will be a substitute for being in the office.

Pre-COVID-19 remote workers found, in contrast, that working from home was in addition to work in the office. Another important aspect of pre-COVID work-from-home is that even though companies had policies permitting it, the ability to do so was still at the discretion of local managers.[61] Given this, it is understandable that organization culture appears to be more important to a good work-life balance than specific company policies.[62]

The Evidence So Far: Who Wins in Work-from-Home?

Arguably the most influential study on pre-COVID remote work has been a field experiment looking at individual contributors in a call center in China, where the researchers were able to get an employer to run an experiment that randomly assigned employees to different treatments.

Half were sent to work from home while half stayed in the office. Productivity was 13% higher for those employees working from home, in large part through being able to work longer, taking up the savings from not commuting. The real-estate savings from shutting down office space for half the workers could have been substantially more. The researchers extended the study to allow workers to self-select whether to stay home or come back to the office. The split was roughly even. They found that productivity jumped even further. Not everyone was equally able to work from home, which is a reminder that telework is not for everyone.[63] This study shows the most positive benefits from remote work—especially, but not only, real-estate savings.

Another call center study designed carefully used applicant responses to job advertisements with different attributes and found that applicants on average would take 8% less pay in a job that allowed them to work from home,[64] an issue we see some employers trying to exploit (more on that later).

A final call center study suggests the many avenues through which performance effects could take place, not all of them good. On the one hand, the researchers found that when employees who had been at the office were allowed to work remotely before the pandemic, at least one measure of their productivity jumped significantly. When all employees had to work remotely, the productivity of those who had remained in the office jumped as well. Over time, though, the remote employees were substantially less likely to be promoted (12% less). But when the call center hired new workers into remote positions, their performance was significantly worse (18%) than those who were hired into jobs on-site. Exactly why is not clear. Whether the applicants were different (as the authors suggest) or whether the selection process was different for the two types of positions is not clear.[65]

The caveat to the implications of these studies for contemporary work-from-home questions is that call center jobs are virtually all individual contributors working on their own computers with little or no need to interact with each other. They could just as easily have been independent contractors.

The most unusual context and thoroughly studied example of remote work is arguably in the federal government, in the US Patent Office. It was initiated in 2012 by the Telework Enhancement Act Pilot Program. It is interesting to note the foresight of the federal government in this case. The idea here was for employees to work permanently anywhere they wanted, cutting office space—$52 million just in 2019—but also improving retention, increasing productivity, and making the hiring process easier. The Patent Office calculates that it saved $120 million in total from the program in 2019.[66]

Interestingly, the Patent Office already had telecommuting programs. One such program was the Patents Hoteling Program, in which employees could work from home and then show up at headquarters twice each pay period for check-ins. This allowed for the sharp reduction in offices and real estate. A "hoteling" model of shared space is discussed in more detail below. (A further benefit of the program for the government was no "snow days.")[67]

A careful and independent study looked at both the telecommuting or "work from home" program and the permanent relocation or "work from anywhere" program.[68] It found that there was an additional increase in employee performance in moving to the work-from-anywhere model from the original work-from-home model. What is perhaps most important in the results is some evidence that the reason for the improvement was fundamentally psychological, something like reciprocity in return for receiving this benefit of not having to go into an office or be constrained at all as to where they lived.

The advantage of this study is that it has very clear and objective measures of job performance in white-collar jobs that are highly skilled. The disadvantage for our purposes is once again that the context is not traditional office work. Almost all of the Patent Office jobs are also individual contributor roles, where there is little need to interact with each other.

One might wonder why the Patent Office had such forward-thinking programs. First, patent examining work requires lawyers and subject matter experts who are otherwise hard to attract and retain at government wage levels, so there was a need to find other, better attributes to attract them. Second, the work is quite individualized and also standardized, which makes it easier to measure and monitor. Third, the patent examiners and other professionals are unionized and could push for changes their members wanted.

A study in the context of more typical administrative office work looked at a more modest form of working from home, where employees could decide when to start and stop their day and where to do their work one day a week. They decided this in advance so that it was part of the office schedule. This was part of a European Union effort called Smart Working, where the goal is to improve the quality of working life for employees and help them deal with work-life balance issues. The study found, perhaps not surprisingly, that 98% of workers chose Friday as their smart workday. Employees who had this option reported better health, fewer sick days, and also better performance, including as measured by their supervisors.[69]

It is important to note that one of the biggest factors in reducing stress-related health problems and improving well-being is to give employees control. How many of the benefits we see should be attributed to the time off per se, and how many due to greater employee control, is hard to parse, but we know that both matter. More generally, a crucial aspect of work-from-home is that most employers gave employees considerable control as to what they did over the course of the day.

Remote Shift: Points to Remember

We can sum up what prior research has told us about the conditions that make remote work effective, at least from the perspective of individual job performance:

- Far and away the best predictor of whether employees will be productive and successful working remotely is how *independent* the tasks they need to perform are from what others in the organization have to do.
- The more collaboration is required in a job, the more challenges there are to doing it remotely. This problem does not go away with video meetings.
- Agile project management, with its demands of constant feedback, face-to-face communication, and real-time testing, is especially difficult to do remotely.

- Generally, the more telework an individual does, the less engaged they are.
- Virtual teams have more conflicts than in-person teams.

Employers that choose the path of remote work must put in extra effort to make it succeed. Those efforts include the following:

- Constant communication with remote workers about business and office developments.
- Remote work transfers even more tasks onto supervisors.
- Figuring out team dynamics is even more challenging in remote environments, where the team has less opportunity to work things out on its own.
- IT becomes much more crucial. And the cybersecurity issues associated with remote work are staggering.
- Almost everything we know about remote work is based on employees who had been in the office and then transitioned to working remotely. We have very little idea of how employees who have never been in the office—let alone any office—will perform in a remote setting.

Chapter 3

How Remote Working Alters the Future of Work

Until the pandemic, Facebook was paying employees a bonus to live close to its headquarters. Now, it is largely leaving the choice up to employees, with the caveat that they receive approval for remote work. That's a big change. In noting what this means for the future, Zuckerberg gave a new reason: the ability to hire differently.

"One [benefit] is access to a wider talent pool. So right now, we're constraining ourselves to a small number of cities. It hasn't been *too* bad of a constraint, but certainly there's an advantage to opening up more widely," he said.[70]

In short, if employees can work anywhere, we can hire them anywhere. Being able to hire from a broader pool applies to permanent work-from-home arrangements. While the benefits to employers are told from the perspective of getting access to better applicants, it is hard not to believe that expanding the supply, other things being equal, also leads to lower wages.

Does the virtual approach mean that we have to stop at our national borders when it comes to employing and hiring workers? If we want to hire workers from a foreign country, they need visas that allow them to work in the United States, and those are limited. If they work for us remotely, however, that is no longer the case. Foreign citizens living in other countries do not need a visa or work permit to be hired by a US company as long as they do not do any of their work in the United States. Income earned by a non-US citizen living and working abroad is not taxable in the United States. A US company with a permanent work-from-home program could hire employees in any country.

Being able to hire people who would otherwise not want to relocate sounds great for employers unless their competitors do the same thing with their employees. In that case, their workforce also has opportunities that are unbound by location. Just as there are more possible candidates for your openings, your employees also have many other places where they could work without having to relocate. If you think your employees are job-hoppers now, wait until they can change employers without relocating.

What we know about retention matters as well: The single most important factor holding people in organizations is social relationships. The more virtual we are, the more we and our colleagues are remote workers, the less we see of each other, and the less of that hold we have. Employees won't be staying because they like the location or because of office perks if there is no office. Social relationships weaken when we don't see people. Other than the work we do and the money, little else holds us in place.

If your organization goes to an all-remote workforce and competitors do not, then this approach might work. The reverse would certainly be bad, to be the only employer hiring locally when your employees could be recruited from everywhere. If everyone moved in that direction, things could be radically different in ways that are hard to imagine: a fluid workforce constantly churning through with nonstop hiring to backfill nonstop turnover.

It is also possible that employee interest in working from home may drive employers in that direction, especially in labor markets that are well organized and where employees have good information on what competing employers are offering. We can already see some evidence for this. One example is the hiring of associates into law firms, which happens at scale, all at once, every spring. Graduates from the same schools interview at many of the same firms, and they all share information. In Philadelphia, law firms report that the 2021 graduates are asking potential employers about their work-from-home policies. It is apparently a good job market for graduates, and the firms say that they feel some competitive pressure to offer generous policies in order to attract the best candidates.

The most likely benefit for employers is that permanent work-from-home arrangements may help retain employees who really want to keep working from home. If we think our competitors in the labor market are already going in that direction, it could make sense to get ahead of the market and begin offering some of those benefits. But this assumes that remote work is actually better for job and organizational performance, or at least not worse.

Will Employees' Pay Suffer?

One of the stranger and more contentious issues in the work-from-home debate is whether it should change the criteria used to set pay. Specifically, will your zip code shape how much you are paid? The argument is that you should be paid based on the cost of living where you live, and if you move to a cheaper place, you should be paid less. Facebook and Twitter announced this policy early on in the pandemic. Stripe offered to give employees a $20,000 bonus if they would move to a cheaper location and then take a 10% wage cut. Silicon Valley companies were expecting employees to take about a 15% pay cut if they moved.[71]

Here's why none of this really makes sense in the current moment: Silicon Valley programmers and IT people are highly skilled and fit the unique needs of the companies where they are working right now. If your company did not pay them their current wage, someone else would. You are paying that wage because the market dictates it, not because the Bay Area is an expensive place to live. Bankers in New York get paid a lot because of the work they are doing, not because New York City is more expensive than, say, Charlotte, North Carolina, where banking jobs are very different. In fact, one of the reasons New York City and Silicon Valley are expensive places to live is that people there get paid a lot of money and can bid up the price of housing, which is the main cost-of-living difference.

Unlike the cost-of-living adjustments that companies used to pay when managers were assigned to different locations, the companies that are thinking about paying employees based on where they live are not requiring any of those employees to live where they do. Suppose, for example, that your company has its headquarters in Silicon Valley, where real estate is very expensive, and one of your employees decides to move their family out to the Central Valley of California, where housing is much cheaper, and commute. Would you cut their pay? Should they be paid less than someone who pays a lot for a tiny house in Los Gatos but has no commute? It's their choice. If the CEOs of these companies decided to work from their ranch in Wyoming, I am certain there would be no effort to cut their pay. If you were contracting work from a consultant, you would not expect the price to vary based on where their home is.

The idea that we should *encourage* our employees to live someplace cheaper so that we can pay them less seems irrational. If they move to Stockton to be with their families, they get a pay cut because housing is cheaper there; but if they move to Aspen, where housing is more expensive, their pay stays the same or even increases? Again, we aren't paying Silicon Valley programmers a lot because housing is expensive there. We are paying them a lot because they are really good, we want the best, and if we didn't pay them their value in the market, someone else would. The fact that programmers in Wyoming get paid less than those in Silicon Valley is irrelevant because they aren't doing the same work and are highly unlikely to have the hot skills we want.

It is also something of a myth to suggest that employees in expensive locations would love the opportunity to live someplace cheaper. I have yet to hear one Wharton MBA student wax eloquently about the incredible value represented by four-bedroom rancher in Iowa versus tiny condos in New York City. There may be people with families who really feel they need space that they cannot afford and are willing to move away from their work to do it, but this is surely not everyone. Interestingly, the companies pushing employees to move are not themselves talking about moving their operations and their leaders to cheaper locations. They just want their employees to do it.

There is one possibility as to why some employers are trying to pay employees less if they move, and it has nothing to do with the cost of living. It is the ability to extract a price from employees who would be willing to pay to live elsewhere. Rather than say that there is a 10% tax on working remotely, we say that your pay will be lowered to the cost of living where you work, which doesn't sound so manipulative. We saw evidence from research in previous chapters that many employees appear willing to pay a price to work from home, and presumably some will pay a bigger price to work from home permanently.

Working from home has sparked another conversation about the future of pay that may be more explicit outside the United States but is sub rosa here. It is about the inappropriateness of jobs being structured around a time clock, with one conversation driven by employees and the other by employers. Like two parallel lines, they never intersect even though they are talking about the same thing.

The Adecco international survey featured in chapter 1 of 8,000 office workers and their bosses reports both employees and executives saying that we should move away from work being based on certain hours sitting at your desk and move toward what the business actually needs.[72]

The problem, though, is that those two groups appear to have completely different ideas as to what that would mean. White-collar workers in the United States, who do not have any overtime restrictions on hours, already know that business needs can go up and up and up, pushing well past the nine-to-five schedule, especially if the work can be done outside the office. The European respondents might want to check in with their US colleagues before heading down that path.

Worries About Burnout

I don't want to suggest that employers have no interest in doing things that will benefit only their employees, but all employers have nagging voices in their investor community, sometimes on their boards, wanting to know how decisions are going to help them and their profitability. At a minimum, they want to know what it might cost if there are no net benefits for the operation. Aside from real-estate savings, what will employers get out of employees working from home?

One idea is that employees who are not commuting have more time that could be spent working, as some of the evidence presented in this and earlier chapters suggests. I suspect employees are thinking that work-from-home will mean the same amount of work done from home and not more work, although the latter has been the case.

Evidence from Gallup surveys in the United States shows that employee perceptions that they are "burned out" have been rising since 2016 and continued to be high in 2020, with the surprising statistic that remote workers reported a higher degree of burnout than those working on-site. The good news for advocates of occasional work-from-home is that before the pandemic, the ability to work from home was associated with reduced perceptions of burnout.[73] If working from home was a way to get away from work pressures, this was impossible to do when there was no choice but to work from home. It is arguably not good news for those wanting to be permanently remote.

There is more systematic evidence on what employees working from home during the pandemic thought about it from countries other than the United States. The results vary: In France, for example, the sense of well-being actually improved during the pandemic in part, researchers believe, because of the comparison effect. Respondents could see what was happening to people elsewhere who lost jobs and felt good about where they were. In Germany, respondents who were working from home appeared to feel less satisfied with their work and family life. And in the UK, respondents mainly felt the same as those in Germany, but relationships with family got marginally better, especially with younger children.[74] All this suggests that the social context of work and family before the pandemic, which varies across countries, affects our assessments a lot. For example, if I had good child care before the pandemic, having to work at home with day care closed was hard because I am trying to work with my kids there. If I had irregular and unsatisfactory day care, being home with my kids might seem like an opportunity to have them safe and cared for. It is very difficult to extrapolate how remote work would have felt without the pandemic context, but that is what we need to assess in order to make the right decisions.

Two Hybrid Work-from-Home Approaches

The results suggest two quite different approaches to remote work. The first is a two-tier model, where one set of employees is permanently remote and the other set is in the office. In the second approach, all or almost all employees have the opportunity to occasionally work from home when they want.

The Two-Tier Hybrid Model

The first type, which I call the Two-Tier Hybrid Model, is the simpler of the two, and we can be reasonably certain about the consequences. The permanently remote workers will become like second-class citizens, something more than contractors but less than the insiders who have direct access to leaders, inside knowledge, and opportunities. We know from prior research that those at home will have fewer opportunities for career advancement and are more likely to be laid off. They will also be Zooming in remotely for any collaborative work, which means projects with them will not be face-to-face.

The Two-Tier model of remote work makes much bigger demands on supervisors of remote employees—anticipating problems they may face from the rest of the office, running interference for them in getting resources, dealing with permissions, and more. Performance management becomes more complicated as well because the day-to-day checking in is more difficult. It becomes much more like managing contractors: more explicit up-front negotiations to reach agreement on expectations and deliverables, much less making changes on the fly. In fact, employees taking the permanent work-from-home option should not be too surprised at some point if the issue of turning them into contractors gets raised.

This type of remote work may have as much similarity to independent contracting as it does to regular employment. One lesson for employers about independent contractors is that they require a fair amount of management time and attention, especially in setting up the project initially and identifying what the performance outcomes will look like. Dropbox decided against adopting a hybrid work-from-home model because of this concern that it would create a two-tier workforce divided between the insiders who are in the office and the outsiders who are not. Interestingly, the company's choice so far has been to keep everything virtual.[75]

But the savings are clear from this hybrid model. We get office space back from our employees, and we can cut it from the budget along with proportionately everything we do for those employees at the office, from parking spaces to coffee and food.

The Choose-Your-Own Hybrid Model

The second type of hybrid model, which more employees want, is where they can choose when and how much to work from home. Let's call it the Choose-Your-Own Hybrid Model. This one is much harder to pull off in terms of administration. As noted earlier, many employees have already been working from home occasionally, often in a manner that is an informal deal with the local manager. Denise Rousseau at Carnegie Mellon University refers to these arrangements as "I-Deals" and reported, many years before the pandemic, that they are quite common.[76]

Many companies have announced that they will give this model a try. Citigroup, for example, says employees will be in the office only three days a week. CEO Jane Fraser also outlined a change in culture going forward, that the assumption will be that there is a good reason when we want everyone in the office at the same time,[77] although the company has yet to announce when employees will return.

The accounting companies are already competing with each other on this front. PwC in the UK announced that once employees come back, they will end the workweek on Fridays at noon in July and August 2021 and then allow employees to work two days a week from home, starting and stopping whenever they like.[78] KPMG essentially matched that policy, cutting two and a half hours off the workweek through the summer and then cutting two days a week from the office. Deloitte is closing four of its offices and telling employees at those offices that they can work from home permanently. BP has told its employees the same thing: They may work two days a week at home.

In the Choose-Your-Own Model, Scheduling Gets Complicated

When we move from opportunities based on the discretion of one's boss to an arguably fairer and more objective policy that gives all employees the right to work from home, things quickly get complicated. Does everyone get to work from home? Many companies are talking about making this option contingent on job performance. Some aspect of job performance was a common requirement in the telecommuting days. For some employees, this option is such a huge benefit that they will make a fuss if they cannot get it.

Part of the fuss is adverse-impact claims. Many people in the United States have some ability to make such claims, based on gender, age, race, religion, disabilities, and more—and rightly so, as local supervisors routinely make decisions based at least in part on such biases. The burden will fall to employers to show that their decision on work-from-home policies was not based on some protected class. It will likely become a full employment plan for lawyers.

Another issue is scheduling when people can work from home. It is far more useful for employees if they can pick the days to accommodate issues at home. Suppose, though, that everyone wants to work from home on the same days in offices where everyone cannot be out at the same time, like the day before a holiday. How will we handle that?

Suppose we try to get back to practices such as agile project management, where we want everyone together to work on some project. Will that overrule our work-from-home schedule, or will we try to make do with some people Zooming in? To some extent, this happens already with vacation days and paid time off (PTO) and sick days, but if everyone gets to work at home one or two days a week, coordinating a project becomes a much bigger challenge.

Robert Pozen and Alexandra Samuel, the authors of *Remote, Inc.*, suggest one option, and that is for work teams to take work-from-home days all at the same time.[79] Doing so could solve the scheduling problem. Apple has announced such a policy, with required office days on Mondays, Tuesdays, and Thursdays and work-from-home options on Wednesdays and Fridays. It does mean that individual employees lose control over the days on which they can work remotely. It also requires that projects be organized such that independent tasks can all be done at the same time, on the same days. Working from home on Friday is great if you happen to have a report that needs to be written then, but if that gets delayed and we are still in deep project mode, work-from-home Friday just means we are all trying to interact via Zoom. Facebook noted this problem and decided not to mandate which days employees would be in the office.

This illustrates the fundamental tension: whether the goal of work-from-home is to benefit individual employees or to benefit the organization.

There are two potential solutions. One is sophisticated algorithms that vendors are likely cooking up as we speak, where members of the team submit their preferences perhaps as short as a week in advance for when they would like to be home, constraints can be added (such as an all-hands meeting on Thursday), and we try to give everyone the schedule that most suits their preferences.

A simpler model with a long track record of success is flextime, where the team negotiates the schedule itself. This requires some initial work in which the employees learn how to negotiate compromises, but once it gets going, it works well, employees like it, and supervisors do not need to get involved. Software has gotten more popular not because it is better or even because it is cheaper but because it requires less from managers and appears to optimize performance.

We can imagine other, simple solutions that benefit both employees and the employer and could be implemented now even without hybrid models. The first of these turns on what many companies have been experiencing during the pandemic: that they cannot get their employees to take vacation or PTO days. This is not a completely altruistic concern about the welfare of employees by the companies, because where employees accrue those days, they sit as liabilities on the organization's financial accounts. If they aren't used, they weigh down the balance sheet.

Why aren't employees taking sick days or PTO days during the pandemic? It could be that we are not as sick as much, and there is some truth to that, as illustrated by the fact that COVID-19 precautions also reduced the number of flu infections. It is also the case, though, that many of us stay home when we are not that sick to do at least some office work. We could be staying home because we are infectious, but we could work if we didn't have to make the commute. If we can work from home, we don't need to take a sick day. The work gets done, and there is no need for a liability of an accrued day on the balance sheet.

When we are working from home, we may not need a PTO day if we have something that requires us to stay home, such as a sick relative. Say we have a doctor's appointment that will likely take a good part of the morning. We could work after that, but by the time we commuted into the office and back, it would hardly be worth it. If we could work from home, we could get back to work for the rest of the afternoon. In those cases, work-from-home days are substitutes for PTO days without the expense to employers.

A thorny issue for employers but a possible benefit for employees is state and local income taxes. Forty-one states have their own income taxes, and 17 of those allow local governments to impose their own taxes. Employers already have to figure out how much tax to withhold based on each employee's residence, something that will get more complicated if work-from-home employees move farther away. The new question has to do with "convenience of employer" rules, which means that you may not have to pay taxes in the jurisdiction where your job is based if your employer requires that the work be performed elsewhere, such as your home. There will be a lot of pressure on employers from their employees to say that work-from-home policies are for the benefit of the employer—and a lot of pushback from tax officials if they do.

Remote Shift: Points to Remember

The COVID-19 remote-work experience leaves us with these conclusions for leaders and managers who have to decide what to do:

- The fact that remote office work is perceived to have gone far better than we expected shuts down managers who simply assumed that no one would do anything if we let them work from home. This creates an opening for experimenting.
- Employers gain in a very clear way from the Two-Tier Hybrid Model remote work, permanent work-from-home, by cutting office space and possibly pay. Employees will pay a potentially big price for permanent remote work and the ability to live away from their office if they want.
- The Choose-Your-Own Hybrid Model of remote work is the reverse. There are many clear benefits to employees, and the more choices they have in deciding when to work from home, the better for them. The benefits to employers are not so clear, given that the approach to save on real estate—hoteling—has not worked well in the past.
- Even modest amounts of occasional work-from-home benefit employees.
- The benefits to employers from remote work during the pandemic in terms of performance seem to be related to

a high-trust approach from management. The alternative of high monitoring and low trust would destroy the main benefit of remote work for most employees, and that is control over what they do and when.

- The more control employees have over when they can work from home and how often, the more complicated the scheduling challenges are for employers.

Chapter 4

Managing the Transition
The Importance of Planning

D espite the backing up by some employers and the delays in getting started, the tea leaves suggest most employers are going to try the work-from-home agenda. But this view is not universal, and it is in flux.

A Gartner survey of employers found that 82% of respondents said they expected their employees to be working remotely for at least some time after the pandemic, and 47% said they expected them to do so full-time.[80] A Mercer survey found reasonably similar results, with 72% of employers expecting to see increased flexibility around when and where work is done, and one-third of employers saying that they expected at least half their workforce to be remote after the pandemic.[81] Put differently, only 11% of employers in a recent Conference Board survey reported that they expect all their employees to return to work after the pandemic subsides, and about a third say that 40% or more of their workforce will be "primarily remote" employees.[82] The largest employer in the United States, the federal government, announced that it will begin allowing its employees work-from-home opportunities in the summer of 2021.[83]

Not every employer is heading toward a work-from-home agenda or sitting on the fence, though. In addition to the investment banks, Amazon alerted its office employees emphatically that it intends to bring everyone back by the fall of 2021 and not pursue a hybrid approach.[84]

The most credible evidence as to where employers are heading might come from what they are doing with their office real estate. Cutting office space would support claims that we will have more remote employees. The most dramatic example early in the pandemic was REI's decision to sell its new headquarters campus just before it was set to move into it last summer. Around the same time, Ralph Lauren and CVS announced plans to cut their office space by 30%.[85] Wells Fargo, for example, has a goal of cutting its footprint by 20% by 2024.[86]

There are also examples where the early enthusiasm to use remote work to cut real estate seems to have cooled. A global survey of CEOs by KPMG found in August 2020 that 69% said that their companies were going to reduce office space because of remote work. But six months later in the spring of 2021, a follow-up survey found that it had fallen to just 17%.[87] While the major tech firms were talking about permanent remote work, in the spring of 2021 they were snapping up huge office-space leases at discount prices with New York City being the prime location. All the major tech companies expanded their footprints in New York during the pandemic.[88] When REI sold its new headquarters, that headquarters was bought one month later by Facebook, one of the companies we think is leading the charge for more permanent remote work.

If we look at what CFOs think—they are watching the purse—a spring 2021 PwC survey found them saying the number one factor they saw as making their business better in the future was "work flexibility," which relates to remote work. In terms of policies for getting the workplace going again, 54% said they were planning to make remote work permanent, and 35% added that they were reducing their real-estate footprint.[89] It was telling that Twitter had its CFO, not its head of HR, talking to the media about the benefits it saw from remote work.[90]

Virtually all companies are planning to bring at least some employees back to the office, which means that almost no employers so far are interested in a completely remote workforce or a completely on-site one. In other words, it is not novel to be thinking of a hybrid model. Every employer is.

One of the most interesting moves has been at IBM, which reported more than a decade ago that 40% of its employees were working remotely on a near-permanent basis. Then, in 2017, it brought many of them back to the office because of the benefits of face-to-face interaction in agile teams. Now it reports that as many as 80% of employees will be able to have some type of work-from-home arrangement after the pandemic. The big difference is that unlike the earlier period of remote work, IBM is not expanding permanent remote workers, who will be about 10% of the workforce.[91]

Onboarding 2.0

Bringing even some employees back to the office after a year and a half, and doing it well, will be a challenge and requires some management. Think of this as onboarding 2.0.

The first issue is safety. Even after restrictions are lifted, many employees will be nervous about returning. Exactly how long to wait and how "normal" the situation should be before bringing back employees is a tough judgment call that depends in part on how well we think things are going now.

The big question with respect to safety is whether businesses will require all returning employees to be vaccinated. Most employers said early on that they would not require employees to be vaccinated. Given the politicization of this particular vaccination, that was a smart position to take, even though I believe virtually all employers will require it for employees who return. It is smarter to wait and let societal pressures work to get the vaccination rate up on its own. It is easier to push a mandate on, say, 10% of the workforce.

As is often the case with new legal topics, the administrative agencies and the courts have said employers cannot tell employees that they *can* mandate vaccinations. But these agencies and courts have suggested that relevant laws will not prohibit them from doing so. In December 2020, the US Equal Employment Opportunity

Commission stated that as long as employers offer reasonable accommodations to those with serious medical or religious reasons for not being vaccinated, federal civil rights laws do not preclude employers from mandating COVID-19 vaccines.[92]

On the other side of the ledger, the Occupational Health and Safety Act requires that employers provide a safe working environment for employees. Consider this problem: If I am particularly at risk from COVID-19, even if I have been vaccinated, is it safe for me to work closely with people who are not vaccinated, and what is the risk to the employer if I do get sick? Such problems begin to limit where the unvaccinated can work. At the same time, another set of laws and ethical concerns prevent employers from identifying who is not vaccinated, although if employers require those not vaccinated to wear masks at work, as it appears that many are planning, it makes identification clearer.

We already experienced a great deal of employee discomfort among essential or on-site workers in trying to learn who had been infected—and when—during the height of the pandemic. Employers are certainly in a bind, as employees have a right to know what kind of exposure they may have had, and other employees certainly have a right to privacy about their medical conditions.[93] The only way around all this is if almost everyone is vaccinated.

In February 2021, a survey of employers found that 48% said they would not mandate vaccines for employees, and 43% said they were still unsure what to do. Seventy-nine percent reported that their concern about mandating vaccines was about employees who would simply refuse to get vaccinated.[94] In this context, which most employers are following, the smart approach is to nudge employees to get vaccinated. Most employers are offering employees PTO to get vaccinated. Some, like Amazon, are offering a bonus, and many more are making the case as to why it is safe and responsible.

In January 2021, the CEO of United Airlines announced the intention of having all its employees be vaccinated as soon as a vaccine became available. He encouraged other employers to follow suit, but none did, and United appeared to waffle a bit on its intentions as it waited to see what everyone else would do.[95] Then in May, Delta followed. Other airlines have now announced that they will not hire candidates who are not vaccinated. My employer, the University of Pennsylvania, said it would require all students to be vaccinated upon their return to campus (many universities have suggested a similar policy), and all faculty and staff must be vaccinated as well. Look for other universities and colleges to follow.

Making the Case for Coming Back

Bringing employees back will not necessarily be a turnkey transition. Among other things, not everyone who was there a year and a half ago will still be there, remembering that hundreds of thousands of people in the United States died from COVID-19. Some of those coming back to the office likely lost friends and relatives to the pandemic. A year and a half is a long time even in normal situations. Employees have retired or moved on, and in some cases, new employees have joined.

We might expect some initial excitement when we get back to the office and see friends again. But we will not exactly pick up where we left off. Not everyone will be in good spirits, and not everyone will be excited about being back to work.

We can think of onboarding 2.0 as having several stages.

1. Explain Why You Are Coming Back

The first stage, before anyone returns, is to explain clearly why you are coming back. This is especially important, because the news has given disproportionate attention to stories about permanent remote options at some companies. Employees need an explanation as to why it is important to come back, why it is necessary for the organization. Without this, it is easy for employees who did not want to come back to think that this is capricious or driven by management bias. In that case, the return will not go well.

An encouraging sign in this direction is that 57% of US employers surveyed by WorldatWork and Salary.com are giving employees information about how their company's finances were affected by COVID-19 as part of their communication efforts. Seventy percent are also providing extra financial support for people with COVID-19 caregiver needs.[96]

2. Talk About What the Pandemic Was Like

The second stage is to acknowledge experiences during the pandemic. Spending some structured time in work groups and teams talking about what it was like trying to work from home and what happened to us during the pandemic humanizes the workplace. It is also an opportunity to transition back to work and to talk about what we learned and what we could do differently going forward. We will come back to the office after a year and a half with somewhat fresh eyes, which allows us to see things differently and to ask whether we still need to do things the same way (like have so many meetings).

3. Help Employees Remember What They Liked About the Office

Other aspects of a return campaign should include highlighting what employees liked about being in the office—perhaps the social connections, or maybe the food—and do more of that, especially at the beginning of the return. The Business Services Group at the University of Pennsylvania is rolling out "Business Services: The Reunion Tour 2021" with return-to-work gift bags the first day back and events for returning employees over the first few weeks. The Graduate School of Education has a "move-in day," during which each returning employee will be met with staff to help them set up their office again, move in any new equipment from home, and get their IT systems up and running. They have also scheduled a staff retreat that will include content on having more effective meetings and alternative ways of sustaining interactions, including virtual sessions with remote employees.[97]

4. Think Carefully About When to Bring Employees Back

Some employers, especially in professional services, are allowing employees who are so inclined to begin coming back to the office immediately, assuming that the numbers are small enough not to violate any restrictions. There is an advantage to this, in that employees who are nervous about returning will eventually come back to an office where everyone is already back working smoothly. The risk, though, is that it can then be more difficult to do any serious reentry and re-onboarding to the post-pandemic workplace if we wait until everyone is back.

The longer we wait for everyone to be back, the less useful these transition events will be for those who have returned. Doing it in waves as people return is certainly better than not doing it at all. Fidelity Investments rolled out a virtual-reality-based onboarding program for new hires during the pandemic.[98] The same technology—bringing people together virtually with their work teams to share experiences—could be done with returning employees before they get back to the office.

Other employers have already announced they will ease employees back into the standard workweek, with schedules like starting back in the office on Tuesdays or late starts in the morning. It is not clear what problem this actually addresses, though. There are advantages in making a cleaner break with the old practices, especially if you want employees to act differently in the office going forward.

What's the Work-from-Home Plan?

As the evidence above suggests, most employers are thinking about some kind of arrangement for occasional remote work. The tech firms may anchor one end of the spectrum with extensive opportunities, while investment banks may occupy the other end with few, if any, opportunities. Whatever it is will require some rollout along with office returns.

Then there is the question of how to actually get work done remotely. Here is where it is useful to have learned lessons from the pandemic. Some companies now have directors of remote work positions, the focus of which is to coordinate lessons and establish rules. GitLab, for example, developed an entire rulebook for online working that includes practices for informal catch-up with employees, hour-long meetings that end after 50 minutes in order to give people a chance for informal talking before the next one, instructions for using Zoom (for real meetings and calls vs. Slack for more informal conversations), and more.[99]

Many employers don't know yet what they want to do. Many seem to want to wait to see what other employers do before they decide. If so, the challenge will be in managing employee expectations. It will be difficult for employees to move from full-on remote to full-on office and then wait to see if some kind of hybrid arrangement eventually emerges. Employees who want remote work in some fashion may jump to another employer rather than wait to see what happens.

Smart employers are already checking in with employees to see what arrangements are important to them and are assessing the trade-offs. IBM has been very effective at engaging employees in online discussions to help craft policies. The drawback of waiting to see what everyone else does is that so far, they are all over the place. There may not be a clear consensus, and it may take a long time before we see patterns that matter. The strategy of waiting looks less and less sensible. Spelling out at least the general principles before employees return is much more sensible than surprising them with a plan after they all return to the office.

Remote Shift: Points to Remember

- Although we thought about returning to the office as a return to normal, having been working remotely for a year and a half feels normal for many people. We had no time or ability to transition from the office to remote work, but we do have time to plan a transition from remote work back to the office.

- Being back in the office will feel different, and as with any change, we need a plan for managing it. This is particularly the case because not everyone will be happy about coming back to the office.
- Treat the return to the office as a massive organizational change that begins with an explanation as to why you are doing it and the plans for remote work. If you plan no expansion of remote work, you need a good explanation as to why.
- The more we can tell employees about our intentions going forward, the better.

Chapter 5

The Opportunity
How to Make Sure We Don't Miss It

Clorox, the manufacturer and marketer of disinfectant products that exploded in demand during the early months of the COVID-19 shutdowns, seized the opportunity of a planned renovation of its Oakland-based headquarters to redirect it. Clorox concluded that remote work seemed to boost morale enough to continue it, so it adjusted the renovation. The company's new plan is to accommodate more collaborative models of work on-site and remotely while facilitating more remote work. It is doing this by eliminating private offices. The new space is planned as a series of private workspaces and meeting rooms that feature collaborative software to engage remote workers. The immediate payoff to the company is to cut its office space by 25%.

Clorox plans to have a group of core employees in the office, a group of permanently remote employees, and schedules for most everyone else to be organized around the needs of their teams. The new norm is to treat remote workers as essential.[100]

Clorox's rethinking highlights the real opportunity for employers to change the way the organization operates—and not just in response to the pandemic. It is an opportunity to make fundamental changes that may have been desired, or needed, for some time.

The idea of a "fresh start" that can motivate us to change directions has been documented around significant landmarks in time, such as the start of a new year.[101] The return to work after more than a year away is an obvious landmark.

A standard challenge in models of organizational change is how to shake people out of their old habits. This is much easier to do now because most of us have been away from the office long enough that some of our old habits have at least been weakened. Employers that are thinking about renovating their office space should do so now, not only because it is easier to do before employees return but also because it will make it easier to shake employees out of their routines. This prompts the question, What do we want to shake these employees *into*? The story at Clorox was about encouraging collaboration. How do we want employees to behave differently going forward, and how do we want the culture of the workplace to be different? In the Clorox case, the new renovation helps do that.

More generally, a program that begins with articulating desired change and the reasons for it, that shows employees what it looks like, and that begins with a core group of employees has a good chance of changing how returning employees feel about the organization and how they behave. This is a once-in-a-lifetime opportunity for employers, and they should think carefully about choosing to ignore it.

Fujitsu, an IT company, is using the pandemic to retool its culture; it is getting rid of the office-centric approach that included long hours and age-based seniority rather than merit. Practices like working hours can change as part of the return to work, setting new expectations about behavior or even explicit rules. Hitachi is on a similar path, announcing that half its employees can now work remotely.[102]

Where We Need to Adapt

Even if we simply move toward more remote work and are not trying to make other changes, it is nevertheless the case that management practices that had been designed around office work need to adapt as well. Some of those changes are not so trivial.

Organizational Culture

We think of organizational culture as the norms and values that tell employees how to behave. They are especially important when formal rules are inadequate and when employees cannot be monitored. We learn culture in part by observation: copying what leaders do, seeing what works, and fitting into the behavior. It helps shape how employees behave when there is no clear rule or guidance, what they do when no one is looking, and how they present themselves in subtle ways that matter to stakeholders.

To make the obvious point, it is difficult to learn culture if we never see other people. Early in the pandemic, some companies that had vacancies waited to hire because they did not think they could onboard employees appropriately in a virtual context and have them pick up the culture. By now, few employers can wait, but it is still a concern. Simply maintaining the current culture in a remote context is a challenge, as figure 5.1 indicates.

It is difficult to see how a work-from-home arrangement will not weaken an organization's culture. The British Chartered Institute of Internal Auditors (not a group one would have guessed would be focused on this topic) concluded in a recent poll of members that the hybrid models represent a significant business risk.

As the group's CEO noted, "It has never been more urgent for businesses to develop strong systems to both identify and mitigate risks to organizational culture, before it becomes a crisis."[103] Underlying that concern is the risk that fraud will be harder to detect.

Hiring a new employee to be a full-time remote worker, the extreme case, is similar to engaging a consultant or independent contractor. We can pass along some tips about sacred cows in the organization that are not in the written rules, but that is about it. The best way, arguably the only way, to counter the problem is with a truly rigorous onboarding program on-site, which teaches, shows, and practices the important company values. Unfortunately, most companies have been cutting back on this experience, increasingly

Figure 5.1. Pause That Remote

Executives think workers should be in the office much more than they might like.

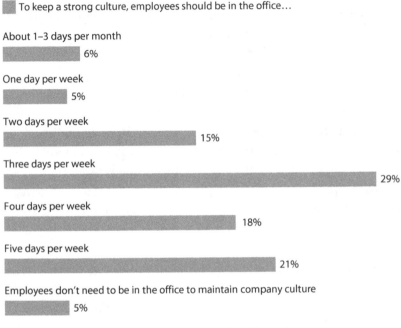

To keep a strong culture, employees should be in the office…

About 1–3 days per month

6%

One day per week

5%

Two days per week

15%

Three days per week

29%

Four days per week

18%

Five days per week

21%

Employees don't need to be in the office to maintain company culture

5%

Source: PwC US Remote Work Survey, January 12, 2021. Base: 133 US executives.
Note: Survey respondents were asked the question "If COVID-19 was not a concern, how often do you think a typical employee needs to be in the office, if at all, in order to maintain a distinctive culture for the company?" Totals do not add up to 100% because of rounding.

moving it online. Imagine how ineffective a remote onboarding experience would be for an employee who is also going to be remote.

The experience is likely to be better, but still tricky, for employees based in the office who work some days on a remote schedule. One reason is that the people they look toward to see the culture are not around as much—the new hire could be remote on any given day, and their mentors and role models could also be remote on any given day. They will eventually get a lot of exposure, but by that time, they likely already think they know how the place operates.

The same is true for experienced hires in workplaces that are in-and-out with remote workers. We simply have less consistent contact with people, weaker social networks, and fewer connections where we update our information and are reminded how to behave. If your organization wants to maintain a strong culture, it will require extra and more concerted efforts, first with onboarding and second with teaching and reinforcing culture with more remote work.

Hiring

Should we think differently about the relevant criteria for hiring candidates if someone will be a permanently remote worker? One issue we need to be much clearer about is to make certain that this is largely an individual contributor role.

The hot topic in hiring in the United States has been the notion of culture fit. (In practice, this criterion often meant hiring people who are like the person doing the hiring.) One might argue it should matter more in a virtual context, where it is more difficult to control the behavior of employees. This approach argues that we should be much more rigorous in defining precisely what values and associated behavior we want and how we will recognize it in candidates. It is certainly less important to care about whether new hires will "fit in" with current employees when they will have only virtual interaction with them.

The argument on the other side is that culture is quite likely to be weaker and less important with remote work, so why worry as much about fit with it. It certainly is less relevant to have a work team be involved in the hiring, given how little face-to-face interaction they may have with the new hire and the fact that most of their decisions seem to come down to first impressions as to whether they like particular candidates. The ability to do the job and to work independently is the key issue.

Pay

In the traditional office context, pay was an emotional topic because it so strongly reflects value and worth in the eyes of the organization, and it was competitive. How our pay compared with that of other people around us mattered in many cases as much as the absolute level of pay. Even when employers had rules that employees were not supposed to discuss pay and before it was clear to them that those rules violated the law, people seemed to find out what others were making.

A more virtual environment means people are less likely to know as much about what other employees are doing and earning. Even if we do learn something about our pay relative to that of others, we do not have the same ability to draw comparisons with what other people are contributing to generate as much inequity. That might reduce complaints, but it also might lead to perceptions of unfairness that are even less valid than the ones in the office setting, where we had at least some sense of how others were performing.

A lot of the arrangements built to try to manage fairness issues will likely fade in importance. Pay structures with grades and step increases that can be earned only for this or that, increases that can be given only once a year, will decline. Expect pay to vary much more even for individuals doing the same work.

Performance Appraisals

Supervisors have done a poor job of administering performance appraisals in recent years. They haven't had the time to do assessments as spans of control have increased and they became individual contributors with their own tasks, as well as supervisors. Assessments tended to be driven by what you could see a subordinate do: Did they volunteer? Were they enthusiastic? Were they in the office a lot? Many of these factors have faded. Peer reviews will be much more difficult to generate as well.

The good news when everyone was working from home during the pandemic is that it was impossible to rely on "face time" as the default proxy for job performance. It's not that people have not tried: Sending messages late at night, for example, is a standard impression management trick. But it does not work as well for impressions as actually seeing people face-to-face. So what did supervisors do? It is important to learn what seemed to work during the pandemic. We hope it was clearer directions about what was expected and how it would be measured.

The move away from formal performance appraisals just before the pandemic began had at its core the idea that continuous conversations and real-time feedback were much better for job performance and indeed all aspects of work than the tick-the-box, form-driven approach most employers had been using.[104] The sense has been that there was backsliding from the feedback approach just before the pandemic because it was easier.

The pressure may well be on to go back to the tick-the-box approach upon a return to the office—especially with permanent remote workers, with whom expectations and assessments will likely become more formal. That would be unfortunate. One of the most important innovations during the pandemic in some organizations was to require that supervisors check in regularly with remote employees, sometimes every week, and simply ask, "How is it going?" This important innovation should flow back from remote work to on-site employees. It is easy for supervisors to assume that because we see our direct reports every day, we know how work is going for them. That is often not the case.

The practice of checking in is a good reminder that it is possible to have social connections even remotely if we are purposeful about them.

Career Development

Formal career development programs do not necessarily have to change for remote workers, but there is a general sense that the informal opportunities for development decline sharply for those who are remote. Is this something we want to accept—that is, if you want to advance, you cannot be a remote employee? That would be much simpler. It is difficult to imagine giving remote workers the kind of leadership experiences that would prepare them in ways similar to on-site employees for bigger jobs, unless those jobs were limited to managing other remote teams.

New Policies Around Eligibility

Existing employees are unlikely to be distributed neatly across job titles such that their interest in working remotely maps onto jobs where that arrangement is most sensible. That means some will really want to work remotely, possibly permanently, but will not be in roles where that makes sense.

As unpleasant as that seems for employees whose role does not match their interest, there is no good way around it. As I explained earlier, making remote work contingent on individual job performance is a tricky exercise. It suggests, among other things, that working from home is a perk and that it involves a high level of trust. If so, then we have unlimited equity issues around who deserves the perk.

That problem exists as well if local managers make the call as to who gets to work remotely and how often. This arrangement never made sense, and it will be even less tolerable after seeing that remote work is more manageable than we thought. Either remote work makes sense for a job or it does not. If the working arrangement varies so much across managers that this principle does not hold, then we need to ask why we have standard job titles at all. Even if we do want to treat work-from-home as a perk, then we need objective criteria for who deserves it.

There is some suggestive evidence that businesses with better management policies going into the pandemic performed better financially.[105] The same is likely to be true going forward.

Remote Shift: Points to Remember

- To paraphrase Winston Churchill (and no doubt others before), never let a good crisis go to waste, because it allows one to do things that could not have been done otherwise. In this case, the pandemic has shaken us out of our office routines, which provides an opportunity to change how we operate there.
- This opportunity will end very quickly if we do not seize it. Any changes we want to make to how we supervise and how we interact and work together, as well as more mundane issues (meetings), should be made as we return.
- As part of the return, we need a re-onboarding program for the first days back to the office.
- Explaining any new work-from-home practices should be part of the re-onboarding program.
- Depending on what those practices are, we need to rethink whether our other management practices need to be adjusted to match. The most important practice to consider systematically is organizational culture. The more remote our new workforce is likely to be, the more effort we need to put into managing our culture.

Conclusion
Looking Past Our Own Offices

This story so far has focused on established companies with a substantial office presence and their decision about moving employees back. What if you don't have an office now? There is a generation of small companies that began operations just before or during the pandemic that never had offices, and there is another cohort of them starting up now. In the past, a goal of these businesses had been to move out of a basement or garage and into an office of their own. Will it still be that way? It may no longer be a badge of respectability to have an established office. Investors may well expect companies to keep working virtually to save money. The right size to need an office has likely been pushed further out.

Remote work after the pandemic may well have a devastating effect on the communities and industries that support office work. It is possible that work-from-home employees will still go out for lunch, although likely less often, and it will be at restaurants near their home, not their office. There is no doubt that restaurants in particular will be hurt by work-from-home practices. It is also possible that the shopping and errands that happen after work will still go on, but again this will likely happen close to home. Some businesses may gain from this, but it seems clearer which ones will lose.

The evidence during the pandemic indicates that people moved from center cities to their suburbs rather than away from their cities to other locales.[106] But this does not tell us much about where they would move post-pandemic or where they will spend their time and money.

The speculation is that cities will lose the most from remote work. But there are good reasons for thinking that long-term work-from-home arrangements will be much worse for the "edge cities" and corporate suburbs. Communities such as Tysons Corner in Virginia or Great Valley outside Philadelphia have huge numbers of white-collar office jobs and, compared with cities, little reason to live nearby other than to be close to the office.

They are likely to be in much worse shape from remote work than cities, because many people want to live in cities, as we now see with the reverse commutes out of them to jobs in the suburbs. Some empty offices there could be converted to condos. I strongly suspect that if we could live anywhere independent of our work, suburbs would suffer the biggest out-migration. If my home is going to be my office, where I will spend much of my time, I might well want to live in a city where there are interesting things to do or in the countryside where there is a great deal of natural beauty.

We often hear the argument that remote work means that employees will be delighted to move away from their expensive housing to cheaper locations, but I doubt that is the case, especially for people without children. Not all employees have that priority, especially those with the elite skills that have employers concerned.

The Event of a Lifetime

The COVID-19 pandemic is the event of a lifetime for modern societies. Unlike all the other "could-be" stories about paradigm-changing phenomena, this one already happened.

The profound question about working from home during the pandemic is whether it suggests that our office orientation for the past 100 or so years has largely been a giant waste of money and time, and that we would have been better off sending employees home to work and saving money on offices and real estate. It is hard to sustain that conclusion given what we know about how remote work operated outside of the system-wide COVID-19 shutdown. Pulling together in a crisis, empowering and trusting employees, was something unique then and likely mattered a great deal, as did the benefit of being able to keep our jobs, do them safely, and take care of our families at a time when many workers did not have that option.

The danger is that leaders will draw the conclusion that offices don't matter, where their priority is just to cut costs, in both real estate and possibly wages. Whether it is possible to repeat our work-from-home performance during the pandemic in a more normal context is an open question. Doing so seems to require a lot more from management than simply sending employees home.

At its core, remote work represents a different way of thinking about office work. We have a lot of experience with the office model, but to paraphrase the writer Rudyard Kipling, those who know only the office know not the office. The comparison with more than a year of remote work has brought it into clearer focus. The fundamental question for employers is, What kind of organization do we want to be?

What typifies a good office working environment includes the following:

- **A strong culture:** We can learn what to do by watching and listening to leaders, and we can also take cues on how to behave from the architecture in well-designed offices. We learn it formally through onboarding programs.
- **High chances of interaction and learning:** We can get questions answered and spark ideas through informal interactions.
- **Control over effort:** Social pressure to perform is greater, because we see more of what other people are accomplishing and also how hard they are working.
- **Good information on context:** We can see whether a particular initiative is important, including informally, from lots of channels, not just approved ones.

The downside is that it's expensive to maintain offices, and commuting to them involves some effort for most employees. Managing employees in the office can be a lot of work, and some of that falls to executives, especially on issues like organizational culture. Many issues that come up, such as perceived inequities, are more common where people work in proximity.

We also have a better idea now of what work-from-home means in comparison with offices. The following are pluses of work-from-home:

- **Savings for employers:** From real estate to associated office perks and even travel, organizations can cut costs.
- **Hiring advantages:** Remote work may be a competitive advantage in hiring and retention, assuming other employers don't adopt the same practices.
- **Savings for employees:** Employees who work at home will not have commuting costs, they will not have to update their work attire, and they will go out to lunch less.
- **More flexibility for employees:** Especially for permanent remote work, employees have more choices as to where they live. Even part-time remote work expands the distance from which we can commute when we need to be in the office. Being able to be home more provides opportunities to solve some work-life challenges.

The downside is that remote employees will lose out compared with those on-site. Workplaces with remote work have less connection to colleagues, lower engagement, less commitment to the organization, and more social isolation. Employers likely have less control over the behavior of employees and their work attitudes. There are fewer opportunities for informal learning and development.

Each extreme requires quite different supporting practices. The biggest mistake is to lean toward one model or the other and not have the practices in place that could make it work.

A serious attempt to run an effective office operation not only requires spending money on real estate and office overhead but also requires effort from managers to make use of the flexible nature of employment, to redirect employees when requirements change, to shape their discretionary effort to get them to act in the interest of the organization, and to manage their interactions to create innovation or other benefits. Employee engagement and commitment to the organization is built in large part on personal ties to peers and leaders, something that happens more naturally in an office setting. If this works well, the sum can truly be greater than the whole of the parts and greater than what individuals could achieve on their own.

The all-remote model is almost the opposite. It is more of a stripped-down model of management that makes it harder to rely on organizational culture and personal ties. Compared with those in the office, remote employees are left alone much more. We specify in advance and in great detail what we want them to do, then wait to see if they do it. The challenge with this is that to make it work effectively requires a lot of trust. The employer has to empower the remote employees to do what needs to be done and figure out when to get it done.

There is much more potential for failure in remote-heavy arrangements. Disengaged employees who do not care about the organization have much more scope to cause damage. It is possible to keep social ties with remote workers, but it requires more purposeful effort. It does not happen naturally. The fact that it was more difficult to micromanage employees working from home during the pandemic created empowerment by default in many organizations, something we should acknowledge and try to replicate.

It is tempting to substitute monitoring employees as a means of ensuring their compliance and performance. As noted above, this is likely to backfire, defeating the flexibility that makes working from home attractive, causing resentment, and reducing the inclination of employees to look out for the organization. Unless employers put in extra effort with remote workers, I suspect they will slide toward a low-trust environment, then to monitoring employees, and eventually to making those remote workers contractors.

I'll leave you with a cautionary tale from the French company Teleperformance. In early 2021, it was reported that the company, with 380,000 employees across 34 countries, is setting up a system to take random scans from webcams to see what its remote employees are doing, a classic low-trust approach.[107] If employees need a break, they will need to enter "break mode" and explain why. They cannot eat during their shift.

This is likely not the experience both employees and employers want to continue in any future—remote, hybrid, or in-office. But with some work, we can all make a better experience for whatever "new normal" we decide.

Acknowledgments

Thanks to Wharton's Center for Human Resources' corporate members for discussions on pandemic-related issues, and to Stewart Friedman and Jack Heuer for comments on the draft manuscript. Thanks also to my editor, Brett LoGiurato, and publisher, Shannon Berning.

Notes

1 Susan J. Stabile, "Google Benefits or Google's Benefit?," *Journal of Business & Technology Law* 3, no. 1 (2008): 97, http://digitalcommons.law.umaryland.edu /jbtl/vol3/iss1/7.

2 Tripp Mickle, "Google Says a Fifth of Workers Will Be Remote Workers," *Wall Street Journal*, May 5, 2021.

3 John T. Cacioppo, Stephanie Cacioppo, Gian C. Gonzaga, Elizabeth L. Ogburn, and Tyler J. VanderWeele, "Marital Satisfaction and Break-ups Differ Across On-line and Off-line Meeting Venues," *Proceedings of the National Academy of Sciences* 110, no. 25 (June 2013): 10135–10140.

4 See, for example, Tsedal Neeley, *Remote Work Revolution: Succeeding from Anywhere* (New York: HarperCollins); and Lynda Gratton, "How to Do Hybrid Right," *Harvard Business Review*, May–June 2021.

5 Chris Gardener, "GMA Correspondent Will Reeve on Getting Caught with No Pants on TV: 'I Have Arrived,'" *Hollywood Reporter*, April 28, 2020.

6 History.com editors, "Spanish Flu," History, May 19, 2020, https://www.history .com/topics/world-war-i/1918-flu-pandemic.

7 Joel Abrams, "How the Devastating 1918 Flu Pandemic Helped Advance US Women's Rights," *The Conversation*, March 1, 2020. For definitive accounts of the Spanish Flu in the United States, see A. W. Crosby, *America's Forgotten Pandemic: The Influenza of 1918* (Cambridge: Cambridge University Press); and L. Spinney, *Pale Rider: The Spanish Flu of 1918 and How It Changed the World* (New York: Public Affairs, 2017).

8 Moira Dickenson, "Marriott Corporate Staff Face Months-Long Furlough," *Wall Street Journal*, March 21, 2020.

9 Emily Stewart, "Corporate America Was Here for You on Coronavirus Until About June," *Vox*, July 24, 2020, https://www.vox.com/covid-19-coronavirus -economy-recession-stock-market/2020/7/24/21334368/pandemic-related-perks -benefits-disappearing-essential-workers-starbucks-covid-19.

10 Olivier Coibion, Yuriy Gorodnichenko, and Michael Weber, "Labor Markets During the COVID-19 Crisis: A Preliminary View" (NBER Working Paper No. 27017, April 2020).

11 "Labor Force Statistics from the Current Population Survey," US Bureau of Labor Statistics, 2020, https://www.bls.gov/cps/effects-of-the-coronavirus-covid-19 -pandemic.htm.

12 Scott R. Baker, Nicholas Bloom, Steven J. Davis, and Stephen J. Terry, "COVID-Induced Economic Uncertainty" (NBER Working Paper No. 26983, April 2020).

13 "Workers Ages 25 to 54 More Likely to Telework Due to COVID–19 in February 2021," US Bureau of Labor Statistics, March 11, 2021, https://www.bls.gov/opub/ted/2021/workers-ages-25-to-54-more-likely-to-telework-due-to-covid-19-in-february-2021.htm.

14 Rakesh Kochhar and Jesse Bennett, "U.S. Labor Market Inches Back from the COVID-19 Shock, but Recovery Is Far from Complete," Pew Research Center, April 14, 2021, https://www.pewresearch.org/fact-tank/2021/04/14/u-s-labor-market-inches-back-from-the-covid-19-shock-but-recovery-is-far-from-complete.

15 Jennifer Liu, "Older Millennials Made It to Management—Now They're Wondering If They Even Want to Be the Boss," CNBC, April 22, 2021, https://www.cnbc.com/2021/04/22/burned-out-millennials-are-rethinking-if-they-want-to-be-the-boss.html.

16 "Resetting Normal: Defining the New Era of Work," Adecco Group report, June 2020.

17 "It's Time to Reimagine Where and How Work Will Get Done," PwC's US Remote Work Survey, January 21, 2021, https://www.pwc.com/us/remotework?WT.mc_id=CT10-PL102-DM2-TR1-LS3-ND30-PR4-CN_ViewpointHighlights-.

18 Louisa Clarence-Smith, "Staff Less Motivated out of Office, Say Company Bosses," *The Times*, September 21, 2020, https://www.thetimes.co.uk/article/staff-less-motivated-out-of-office-say-company-bosses-7qc0c377k.

19 Prodoscore, "2020 Shows Shifting Workday Patterns and Productivity Gains," March 12, 2021, https://www.prodoscore.com/wp-content/uploads/2021/03/Prodoscore-Internal-Data-Shifting-Workday-Patterns-and-productivity-gains.pdf.

20 Michael Gibbs, Friederike Mengel, and Christoph Siemroth, "Work from Home and Productivity: Evidence from Personnel and Analytics Data on IT Professionals" (University of Chicago Becker Friedman Institute Working Paper No. 2021-56, 2021).

21 As quoted in Laura Forman, "The Shift to Remote Work Could Be a Big Swing and a Miss," *Wall Street Journal*, June 6, 2020, https://www.wsj.com/articles/the-shift-to-remote-work-could-be-a-big-swing-and-a-miss-11591452000.

22 "Goldman Sachs: Bank Boss Rejects Work from Home as the 'New Normal,' *BBC News*, February 25, 2021, https://www.bbc.com/news/business-56192048.

23 Natalie Singer-Velush, Kevin Sherman, and Erik Anderson, "Microsoft Analyzed Data on Its Newly Remote Workforce," *Harvard Business Review*, July 15, 2020.

24 Robert I. Sutton, "Remote Work Is Here to Stay: Bosses Better Adjust," *Wall Street Journal*, August 2, 2020, https://www.wsj.com/articles/remote-work-is-here-to-stay-bosses-better-adjust-11596395367.

25 For a review of the evidence on the value of meetings, see Joseph Mroz, Joseph Allen, Dana Verhoeven, and Marissa Shuffler, "Do We Really Need Another Meeting? The Science of Workplace Meetings," *Current Directions in Psychological Science* 27, no. 6 (2018): 484–491.

26 Geoff Tyler, "The Office Citadel Crumbles," *Management Services* 39, no. 9 (1995): 32.

27 See, for example, Mahlon Apgar IV, "Uncovering Your Hidden Occupancy Costs," *Harvard Business Review*, May–June 1993.

28 June Langhoff, "Does Place Still Matter? The Role of the Workplace in a Distributed World," New Ways of Working Network summary, May 1, 2007, http://www.westerncontract.com/wp-content/uploads/Does-Place-Still-Matter .pdf; Nikil Saval, *Cubed: A Secret History of the Workplace* (New York: Doubleday, 2014).

29 C. C. Sullivan, "Earn as You Churn: Minimizing Outlays for Corporate Layouts," *Buildings*, September 1993.

30 Sarah Kessler, "IBM, Remote Work Pioneer, Is Recalling Thousands to Its Offices," Quartz, March 21, 2017, https://qz.com/924167/ibm-remote-work -pioneer-is-calling-thousands-of-employees-back-to-the-office/.

31 Heather Ogilvie, "This Old Office," *Journal of Business Strategy* 15, no. 5 (September/October 1994): 26.

32 Michael Considine and Kurt Haglund, "Reworking the Work Space," *Journal of Management and Engineering* 11, no. 2 (1995): 18–26.

33 An extensive discussion of the Chiat experience is in Warren Berger, "Lost in Space," *Wired*, February 1, 1999.

34 Henry C. Lucas. "Information Technology and Physical Space," *Communications of the ACM* 44, no. 11 (November 2001): 89–96.

35 Kemba J. Dunham, "Telecommuters' Lament: Once Touted as the Future, Work -at-Home Situations Lose Favor with Employers," *Wall Street Journal*, October 30, 2000.

36 Thomas Wailgum, "What Happened to That Whole Hoteling Thing?," *CIO Magazine*, February 15, 2007.

37 "Daily News Roundup: Tuesday, April 20, 2021," BTG Advisory, https://www .btgadvisory.com/news/daily-news-roundup-tuesday-20th-april-2021.

38 Ethan Bernstein and Ben Weber, "The Truth About Open Offices," *Harvard Business Review*, November/December 2019.

39 A review of the situation in 1999 is in Nancy B. Kurland and Diane E. Bailey, "The Advantages and Challenges of Working Here, There, Anywhere, and Anytime," *Organization Dynamics*, Autumn 1999, 53.

40 Kim Parker, Juliana Menasce Horowitz, and Rachel Minkin, "How the Coronavirus Outbreak Has—and Hasn't—Changed the Way Americans Work,"

Pew Research Center, December 9, 2020, https://www.pewresearch.org/social
-trends/2020/12/09/how-the-coronavirus-outbreak-has-and-hasnt-changed-the
-way-americans-work/.

41 For examples, see C. D. Cooper and N. B. Kurland, "Telecommuting,
Professional Isolation, and Employee Development in Public and Private
Organizations," *Journal of Organizational Behavior* 23 (2002): 511–532.

42 For evidence on the former, see W. F. Cascio, "Managing a Virtual Workplace,"
Academy of Management Executive 14 (2000): 81–90; and on the latter, see T. D.
Golden, "Co-workers Who Telework and the Impact on Those in the Office:
Understanding the Implications of Virtual Work for Co-worker Satisfaction and
Turnover Intentions," *Human Relations* 60 (2007): 1641–1667.

43 I am indebted to Rocio Bonet for help with this material, some of which appeared
in Peter Cappelli and Rocio Bonet, "After Covid, Should You Keep Working from
Home? Here's How to Decide," *Wall Street Journal*, March 19, 2021, https://www
.wsj.com/articles/after-covid-should-you-keep-working-from-home-heres-how
-to-decide-11616176802.

44 C. A. Bartel, A. Wrzesniewski, and B. M. Wiesenfeld, "Knowing Where You
Stand: Physical Isolation, Perceived Respect, and Organizational Identification
among Virtual Employees," *Organization Science* 23, no. 3 (2012): 743–757.

45 Kathryn Dill, "WeWork CEO Says Least Engaged Employees Enjoy Working
from Home," *Wall Street Journal*, May 12, 2021, https://www.wsj.com/articles
/wework-ceo-says-workers-who-want-back-into-the-office-are-the-most-engaged
-11620837018; and Elahdi Ezadi, "Washingtonian Staff Goes on Publishing Strike
after CEO's Op-Ed about Remote Work," *Washington Post*, May 7, 2021.

46 Cooper and Kurland, "Telecommuting, Professional Isolation, and Employee
Development in Public and Private Organizations."

47 R. S. Gajendran and D. A. Harrison, "The Good, the Bad, and the Unknown
about Telecommuting: Meta-analysis of Psychological Mediators and Individual
Consequences," *Journal of Applied Psychology* 92, no. 6 (2007): 1524.

48 R. Bonet and F. Salvador, "When the Boss Is Away: Manager–Worker Separation
and Worker Performance in a Multisite Software Maintenance Organization,"
Organization Science 28, no. 2 (2017): 244–261.

49 Andrew Atkinson, "U.K. Says Home Working Held Back Pay and Promotions
Before Covid," *Bloomberg*, April 19, 2021, https://www.bloomberg.com/news
/articles/2021-04-19/working-from-home-in-the-u-k-holds-back-pay-and
-promotions.

50 I. C. Cristea and P. M. Leonardi, "Get Noticed and Die Trying: Signals, Sacrifice,
and the Production of Face Time in Distributed Work," *Organization Science* 30,
no. 3 (2019): 552–572.

51 C. D. Cramton, "The Mutual Knowledge Problem and Its Consequences for
Dispersed Collaboration," *Organization Science* 12, no. 3 (2001): 346–371;

A. Metiu, "Owning the Code: Status Closure in Distributed Groups," *Organization Science* 17, no. 4 (2006): 418–435.

52   Cramton, "Mutual Knowledge Problem."

53   L. Duxbury and D. Neufeld, "An Empirical Evaluation of the Impacts of Telecommuting on Intra-organizational Communication," *Journal of Engineering and Technology Management* 16, no. 1 (1999): 1–28.

54   P. J. Hinds and D. E. Bailey, "Out of Sight, out of Sync: Understanding Conflict in Distributed Teams," *Organization Science* 14, no. 6 (2003): 615–632.

55   Bonet and Salvador, "When the Boss Is Away."

56   T. D. Golden, J. F. Veiga, and Z. Simsek, "Telecommuting's Differential Impact on Work-Family Conflict: Is There No Place Like Home?," *Journal of Applied Psychology* 91, no. 6 (2006): 1340.

57   Golden, Veiga, and Simsek discuss the complications in disentangling the relationships and the difference between the negative impacts that work can have on family life and the negative effects that family life can have on work. They conclude that the former improves and the latter worsens with telecommuting. Golden, Veiga, and Simsek, "Telecommuting's Differential Impact on Work-Family Conflict."

58   Gilles Duranton and Matthew A. Turner, "The Fundamental Law of Road Congestion: Evidence from US Cities," *American Economic Review* 101, no. 6 (2011): 2615–2652.

59   Hamidreza Asgari, Xia Jin, and Yiman Du, "Examination of the Impacts of Telecommuting on the Time Use of Nonmandatory Activities," *Transportation Research Record* 2566, no. 1 (2016): 2566–2579.

60   Mary C. Noonan and Jennifer L. Glass, "The Hard Truth About Telecommuting," *Monthly Labor Review* 135, no. 6 (June 2012): 38–45.

61   Erin L. Kelly and Alexandra Kalev, "Managing Flexible Work Arrangements in US Organizations: Formalized Discretion or 'a Right to Ask,'" *Socio-Economic Review* 4, no. 3 (September 2006): 379–416.

62   Sue Falter Mennino, Beth A. Rubin, and April Brayfield, "Home-to-Job and Job-to-Home Spillover: The Impact of Company Policies and Workplace," *Culture Sociological Quarterly* 46, no. 1 (2005): 107–135.

63   N. Bloom, J. Liang, J. Roberts, and Z. J. Ying, "Does Working from Home Work? Evidence from a Chinese Experiment," *Quarterly Journal of Economics* 130, no. 1 (2015): 165–218.

64   Alexandre Mas and Amanda Pallais, "Valuing Alternative Work Arrangements," *American Economic Review* 107, no. 12 (2017): 3722–3759.

65   Emma Harrington and Natalia Emanuel, "'Working' Remotely? Selection, Treatment, and Market Provision of Remote Work (JMP)" (Harvard University Economics Department Working Paper, 2021).

66   United States Patent and Trademark Office, "Telework Enhancement Act Pilot Program," 2017, https://www.uspto.gov/sites/default/files/documents /TEAPP%202020%20Fact%20Sheet.pdf.

67   This is a simplified description. The Patent Office actually has an array of remote practices for different employees. See "Telework," Patent Office Professional Association, http://www.popa.org/about/work-life-balance/telework/.

68   Prithwiraj Choudhury, Cirrus Foroughi, and Barbara Zepp Larson, "Work-from-Anywhere: The Productivity Effects of Geographic Flexibility," *Strategic Management Journal* 42, no. 4 (2021): 655–683.

69   Marta Angelici and Paola Profeta, "Smart Working: Flexibility Without Constraints" (CES Working Paper No. 8165, 2020).

70   Casey Newton, "Mark Zuckerberg on Taking His Massive Workforce Remote," *The Verge*, May 21, 2020, https://www.theverge.com/2020/5/21/21265780 /facebook-remote-work-mark-zuckerberg-interview-wfh.

71   Katherine Bindley and Eliot Brown, "Silicon Valley Pay Cuts Ignite Tech Industry COVID-19 Tensions," *Wall Street Journal*, October 11, 2020, https:// www.wsj.com/articles/silicon-valley-pay-cuts-ignite-tech-industry-covid-19 -tensions-11602435601.

72   The Adecco Group, Resetting Normal: Defining Work in the New Era, June 2020.

73   Ben Wigert and Jennifer Robison, "Remote Workers Facing High Burnout: How to Turn It Around," Gallup Workplace, October 30, 2020, https://www.gallup .com/workplace/323228/remote-workers-facing-high-burnout-turn-around.aspx.

74   For France, see Ettore Recchi, Emanuele Ferragina, Emily Helmeid, Stefan Pauly, Mirna Safi, Nicolas Sauger, and Jen Schradie. "The 'Eye of the Hurricane' Paradox: An Unexpected and Unequal Rise of Well-Being During the Covid-19 Lockdown in France," *Research in Social Stratification and Mobility* 68 (August 2020): 1–8. For Germany, see Katja Möhring, Elias Naumann, Maximiliane Reifenscheid, Alexander Wenz, Tobias Rettig, Ulrich Krieger, Sabine Friedel, Marina Finkel, Carina Cornesse, and Annelies G. Blom, "The COVID-19 Pandemic and Subjective Well-Being: Longitudinal Evidence on Satisfaction with Work and Family," *European Societies* 23 (2021): S601–S617. For the UK, see M. Benzeval, J. Burton, T. F. Crossley, P. Fisher, A. Jäckle, B. Perelli-Harris, and S. Walzenbach, "Understanding Society COVID-19 Survey May Briefing Note: Family Relationships" (Understanding Society Working Paper No 13/2020, ISER, University of Essex, 2020).

75   "How to Avoid the Return of Office Cliques," *Financial Times*, May 26, 2021, https://www.ft.com/content/c113f86b-fbe3-4ed4-b39a-359ad57d72b8.

76   Denise Rousseau, *I-Deals: Idiosyncratic Deals Employees Bargain for Themselves* (New York: M. E. Sharp, 2005).

77   David Benoit, "Citigroup Plans for Hybrid Workforce Post-Pandemic," *Wall Street Journal*, March 23, 2021, https://www.wsj.com/articles/citigroup-plans-for -hybrid-workforce-post-pandemic-11616519476?mod=article_inline.CEO.

78 "PwC Says Start When You Like, Leave When You Like," *BBC News*, March 31, 2021, https://www.bbc.com/news/business-56591189.

79 Robert C. Pozen and Alexandra Samuel, *Remote, Inc.: How to Thrive at Work . . . Wherever You Are* (New York: Harper Business, 2021).

80 Kathryn Mayer, "HR Leaders Plan to Embrace Remote Work Post-Pandemic," Human Resource Executive, July 20, 2021, https://hrexecutive.com/hr-leaders-plan-to-embrace-remote-work-post-pandemic.

81 Mercer, "Flexing for the Future," July–August 2020 survey, https://www.mercer.us/content/dam/mercer/attachments/private/us-2020-flexing-for-the-future.pdf.

82 "Adapting to the Reimagined Workplace: Human Capital Responses to the COVID-19 Pandemic," Conference Board, April 2020, https://conference-board.org/topics/natural-disasters-pandemics/adapting-to-the-reimagined-workplace.

83 Lisa Rein, "Biden Administration Moves Toward Making the Pandemic Work-from-Home Experiment Permanent for Many Federal Workers," *Washington Post*, May 24, 2021, https://www.washingtonpost.com/politics/federal-employees-working-from-home/2021/05/23/73c34304-b8db-11eb-a6b1-81296da0339b_story.html.

84 Katherine Anne Long and Paul Roberts, "Amazon Expects a Return to Offices by Fall: Some Workers Are Miffed While Nearby Businesses Are Ecstatic," *Seattle Times*, March 31, 2021, https://www.seattletimes.com/business/amazon/amazon-expects-employees-back-in-their-offices-by-autumn.

85 Lauren Thomas, "COVID Changed How We Think of Offices. Now Companies Want Their Spaces to Work as Hard as They Do," CNBC, March 10, 2021, https://www.cnbc.com/2021/03/10/1-year-into-covid-employers-rethink-offices-and-function-matters-most.html.

86 Ben Eisen, "Wells Fargo Plans to Bring Employees Back to the Office in September," *Wall Street Journal*, March 30, 2021, https://www.wsj.com/articles/wells-fargo-plans-to-bring-employees-back-to-the-office-in-september-11617133597.

87 "Major Employers Scrap Plans to Cut Back on Offices—KPMG," Reuters, March 22, 2021, https://www.reuters.com/article/uk-economy-ceos/major-employers-scrap-plans-to-cut-back-on-offices-kpmg-idUSKBN2BF00B.

88 Erica Pandey, "Tech Companies Gobble Up Office Space," Axios, January 27, 2021, https://www.axios.com/technology-companies-office-space-cb7ffed2-b611-4b51-9c7e-3acbe1b1f7a4.html.

89 "PwC US CFO Pulse Survey," PwC, June 15, 2020, https://www.pwc.com/us/en/library/covid-19/pwc-covid-19-cfo-pulse-survey.html.

90 "Twitter CFO Ned Segal, on the Workforce of the Future," *Bloomberg*, December 1, 2020, https://www.bloomberg.com/news/videos/2020-12-02/twitter-cfo-ned-segal-on-the-workforce-of-the-future-video.

91   Brody Ford and Emily Chang, "IBM Sees 80% of Employees Working in Hybrid
     Roles After Pandemic," *Bloomberg*, March 31, 2021, https://www.bloomberg.com
     /news/articles/2021-03-31/ibm-expects-80-of-its-employees-to-work-hybrid
     -post-pandemic.

92   "What You Should Know About COVID-19 and the ADA, the Rehabilitation
     Act, and Other EEO Laws," US EEOC, May 28, 2021, https://www.eeoc.gov
     /wysk/what-you-should-know-about-covid-19-and-ada-rehabilitation-act-and
     -other-eeo-laws. As with all legal issues, there are caveats and exceptions.

93   Josh Eidelson, "Covid Gag Rules Are Putting Everyone at Risk," *Bloomberg
     Businessweek*, August 8, 2020, https://www.bloomberg.com/news/features/2020
     -08-27/covid-pandemic-u-s-businesses-issue-gag-rules-to-stop-workers-from
     -talking.

94   "The Littler COVID-19 Vaccine Employer Survey Report," Littler, February 9,
     2021, https://www.littler.com/publication-press/publication/littler-vaccine
     -employer-survey-report.

95   Gillian Friedman and Lauren Hirsch, "Health Advocate or Big Brother?
     Companies Weigh Requiring Vaccines," *New York Times*, May 7, 2021, https://
     www.nytimes.com/2021/05/07/business/companies-employees-vaccine
     -requirements.html.

96   "Six Months Later: COVID-19 Employer Response Survey, Part 2,"
     WorldatWork, October 20, 2020, https://worldatwork.org/press-room/six
     -months-later-covid-19-employer-response-survey-part-2.

97   Ray Bates and Emma Grigore, respectively, head these two efforts.

98   Sarah Castellanos, "New Hires to the Holodeck: Fidelity Investments Tries
     Collaboration via Virtual Reality," *CIO Journal*, October 8, 2020.

99   Pilita Clark, "Why 'Hybrid' Working Spells Trouble for Companies," *Financial
     Times*, September 22, 2020, https://www.ft.com/content/59c77968-fb28-482f
     -9334-a9960ef6d667.

100 Russ Mitchell, "Less Office Space, More Video Screens: How One Company Is
     Embracing Hybrid Work," *Los Angeles Times*, May 20, 2021, https://www.latimes
     .com/business/story/2021-05-20/clorox-embraces-hybrid-work-trimming-down
     -office-space.

101 Hengchen Dai, Katherine L. Mikman, and Jason Riis, "The Fresh Start Effect:
     Temporal Landmarks Motivate Aspirational Behavior," *Management Science* 60,
     no. 10 (2014): 2563–2582.

102 "Coronavirus Catalyzes Overdue Change in Japan's Offices," *Financial Times*,
     July 22, 2020, https://www.ft.com/content/500a9c04-afeb-11ea-94fc
     -9a676a727e5a.

103 The study is reported in Michael O'Dwyer, "Hybrid Working Makes It Harder to
     Detect Fraud," *Financial Times*, May 28, 2021, https://www.ft.com/content
     /faca3a1a-6704-473d-ba80-f16acb809755.

104 Peter Cappelli and Anna Tavis, "The Performance Management Revolution," *Harvard Business Review*, October 2016.

105 There are several of these studies, which span countries, and their measure of "good" management practices is simply whether they have standard approaches as opposed to informal management winging it. They are reviewed in Andrew Hill, "The Simple Tools That Helped Business Resist the Crisis," *Financial Times*, May 23, 2021, https://www.ft.com/content/5f5f4285-da68-4b02-8895 -bca3c5a8d486.

106 Arjun Ramani and Nicholas Bloom, "The Donut Effect of COVID-19 on Cities" (NBER Working Paper No. 28876, 2021).

107 Peter Walker, "Call Centre Staff to Be Monitored via Webcam for Home-Working 'Infractions,'" *The Guardian*, March 26, 2021, https://www.theguardian .com/business/2021/mar/26/teleperformance-call-centre-staff-monitored-via -webcam-home-working-infractions.

Index

Page numbers in italics refer to figures.

About the Author

Peter Cappelli is the George W. Taylor Professor of Management at the Wharton School and director of Wharton's Center for Human Resources. He is also a research associate at the National Bureau of Economic Research in Cambridge, Massachusetts, and since 2007 is a Distinguished Scholar of the Ministry of Manpower for Singapore.

Cappelli's recent research examines changes in employment relations in the United States and their implications. Cappelli writes a monthly column on workforce issues for Human Resource Executive Online and is a regular contributor to the *Wall Street Journal* and the *Harvard Business Review*. His recent books include *Fortune Makers: The Leaders Creating China's Great Global Companies* (with Michael Useem, Harbir Singh, and Neng Liang); *Why Good People Can't Get Jobs: The Skills Gap and What Companies Can Do About It*; *The India Way: How India's Business Leaders Are Revolutionizing Management* (with Harbir Singh, Jitendra Singh, and Michael Useem); and *Managing the Older Worker: How to Prepare for the New Organizational Order* (with Bill Novelli).

Cappelli has degrees in industrial relations from Cornell University and in labor economics from Oxford, where he was a Fulbright Scholar. He has been a Guest Scholar at the Brookings Institution; a German Marshall Fund Fellow; and a faculty member at MIT, the University of Illinois, and the University of California at Berkeley.

WHARTON
SCHOOL
PRESS

About Wharton School Press

Wharton School Press, the book publishing arm of the Wharton School of the University of Pennsylvania, was established to inspire bold, insightful thinking within the global business community.

Wharton School Press publishes a select list of award-winning, best-selling, and thought-leading books that offer trusted business knowledge to help leaders at all levels meet the challenges of today and the opportunities of tomorrow. Led by a spirit of innovation and experimentation, Wharton School Press leverages groundbreaking digital technologies and has pioneered a fast-reading business-book format that fits readers' busy lives, allowing them to swiftly emerge with the tools and information needed to make an impact. Wharton School Press books offer guidance and inspiration on a variety of topics, including leadership, management, strategy, innovation, entrepreneurship, finance, marketing, social impact, public policy, and more.

Wharton School Press also operates an online bookstore featuring a curated selection of influential books by Wharton School faculty and Press authors published by a wide range of leading publishers.

To find books that will inspire and empower you to increase your impact and expand your personal and professional horizons, visit *wsp.wharton.upenn.edu.*

About the Wharton School

Founded in 1881 as the world's first collegiate business school, the Wharton School of the University of Pennsylvania is shaping the future of business by incubating ideas, driving insights, and creating leaders who change the world. With a faculty of more than 235 renowned professors, Wharton has 5,000 undergraduate, MBA, executive MBA, and doctoral students. Each year 13,000 professionals from around the world advance their careers through Wharton Executive Education's individual, company-customized, and online programs. More than 100,000 Wharton alumni form a powerful global network of leaders who transform business every day.

For more information, visit www.wharton.upenn.edu.